Lore *of the* Dolphin

Tales of Our Connection through the Ages

Edited by Natalia Burns

BEYOND
WORDS
Publishing
I N C

Beyond Words Publishing, Inc.
20827 N.W. Cornell Road, Suite 500
Hillsboro, Oregon 97124-9808
503-531-8700

Managing editor: Julie Steigerwaldt
Proofreader: Marvin Moore
Design: Dorral Lukas
Cover art: Susan Gross
Composition: William H. Brunson Typography Services

Printed in the United States of America
Distributed to the book trade by Publishers Group West

Library of Congress Cataloging-in-Publication Data
    Lore of the dolphin / edited by Natalia Burns.

       p.   cm.
    Includes bibliographical references.
    ISBN 1-58270-086-9
    1. Dolphins—Literary collections.   2. Dolphins.   I. Burns, Natalia.
    PN6071.D64 L67   2002
    80'8.8'0362953—dc21

                                                                  2002005021

The corporate mission of Beyond Words Publishing, Inc.:
    Inspire to Integrity

To my mother, my husband, and my baby.
Without you, nothing would have meaning.

Contents

Part Two: Dolphin Dance 75

Acknowledgments

Thanks from the bottom of my heart to Kate Wiley, Eileen Charbonneau, Gill Braulik, Barney Leason, Karen Leason Pagarani, and Valley Stream's terrific celebrity librarians Elizabeth Costello, Lena Sau, and Joyce Rogawski for all of their help and encouragement in getting this book together. I couldn't have pulled these stories together without my hard-working research assistant and niece Mimi Wilkins Winter or my good friend and longtime ally Syed Ahmed. Thanks also to all the wonderful writers included in this volume, living and dead, who've felt the dolphins' touch and been changed by it.

Cindy Black and Julie Steigerwaldt at Beyond Words made the more difficult parts of finishing this book a pleasure with their generous help, endless energy, and limitless creativity. And this book never would have "hatched" without the efforts, judgment, and vision of my wonderful agent, Susan Crawford. Thank you.

And finally, thank you to the dolphins for the years of comfort and wild inspiration you've given me!

Preface

Welcome to the magical realm of the dolphin. Beloved around the world for their intelligence, beauty, playfulness, and a flattering tolerance for humans, it's no wonder that dolphins fascinate us endlessly. In these pages you'll meet these complex and intelligent "angels of the deep" in their own territory. Some selections might be familiar—others will surprise you.

Our tour of dolphin territory begins at the beginning of time with folktales of dolphin origins—how dolphins were created from humans and how humans were created from dolphins. Moving and evocative, these touching stories come from such distant reaches as Nepal, North Australia—and California. Ancient Greek accounts tell of the compassion of dolphins, who've been seen holding up their dead companions as though to help them breathe. You'll read Chinese tales of a dolphin river goddess, how the image of the dolphin has been used through history, and how that symbolism might have been responsible for getting Galileo into trouble during the Renaissance.

In part two we enter modern times and watch dolphins in action with people today—even though we've lost the companionable closeness we once may have had. But dolphins who transform into human male lovers, who rescue drowning people, or who choose to live among people instead of with other dolphins—these are the stories of today. There's even a story of a dolphin who brings gifts from the sea floor to a couple who rescued her from a bait net!

In part three we'll meet dolphins who help people heal. Can a dolphin send waves of wonderful feeling through the legs of a paraplegic? Or make contact with a brain-damaged child who wants nothing to do with her? How about "diagnosing" a life-threatening infection in a quadriplegic woman who has no idea she's ill? Here are the stories of how these things happened.

So come on in, the water's fine—and bubbling with stories, anecdotes, and poems about our ancient cousins and our timeless connection.

Part One

Dolphin Dawn

From the dawn of storytelling, from the dawn of history, from the dawn of time, dolphins and people have shared a primal bond as electric as the one between Michelangelo's God and Adam. The Ancients tell moving and beautiful legends of humans created from dolphins and dolphins created from humans. Our enduring connection is as old as the chain between ourselves and our most ancient ancestors.

The Bond Cannot Be Broken
A Folktale from Nepal of the Ganges River Dolphin

retold by Brian D. Smith

In the time of the ancients there was a benevolent king named Bhagirath. The king prayed to Lord Shiva for a thousand years to bring a great river to his people. When Shiva was satisfied with the king's devotion he created a wondrous life-giving river from his long flowing hair. To spread the news that the river was coming, Shiva also made the dolphin SuSu and gave him the name Bhagirath after the king who brought the river to the people of Nepal. As the messenger king, the dolphin became husband to the river. This sacred bond between dolphin and river cannot be broken; without a husband there can be no wife. Without the messenger king, who will carry the story of the river?

How Dolphins Came from People
A Chumash Indian Legend

retold by Katharine K. Wiley

Hutash walked alone on the island of Limuw. She spoke with the animals and the trees, but still she was alone. She wanted to share her home with people. So she climbed the highest mountain on Limuw and gathered the seeds of the poppy. She cast the seeds before her. The seeds grew into plants and when they opened they were people, men and women and young and old. This is how the Chumash came to be, and Hutash loved them as her own children.

Hutash's husband, the Sky Snake [the Milky Way] saw the Chumash and he also loved them as his own children. He saw they were cold. So he stuck out his tongue and struck the ground, and fire began to burn.

The Chumash gathered around the fire. They sang praise and thanks to Hutash and Sky Snake.

The Chumash tribe grew and grew. They cooked on many fires and hunted the animals and chanted and danced, even into the night. They made so much noise Hutash could not rest.

Hutash came to the village, but at first the Chumash were all too busy to listen to her. But finally they listened.

Hutash said to them, Limuw has grown crowded. In three days half of the Chumash must leave Limuw and go across the water to the land there. In three days I will make a bridge. Those who have chosen to leave will cross the water on my bridge.

Then Hutash left. The Chumash sat down to decide who would leave Limuw and who would stay.

Three days later a bridge of many colors stood in the sky. It went from the highest mountain on Limuw to the highest mountain on the land across the water. The families that had chosen to leave Limuw climbed up and began to cross the rainbow bridge.

On the way, some of the Chumash began to wonder. How could they walk through the sky on a bridge of colors? What held them up? But when they looked over the side they lost their balance and fell. They fell out of the sky and down into the sea.

Hutash saw them falling, Hutash heard them crying out. The Chumash were as her children to her, and she did not want them to drown. So Hutash made them into dolphins that leap and dance in the sea.

How People Came from Dolphins
An Aboriginal Story from North Australia

Amanda Cochrane and Karena Callen

In the very early days, the Earth was inhabited by spirit beings who took the forms of animals, birds and fishes. Some of these first ancestors were called the Indjebena, the dolphins. They were smaller than the dolphins we know today, and led a happy, carefree life, spending most of their day in play. In those days the wisest creatures in the ocean were the yakuna, the bailer shells. They possessed exquisite shells and spent most of their time creeping slowly along the ocean floor looking for tiny creatures to feed on.

Dinginjabana, leader of all the dolphins, was very strong, bold and agile. His mate, Ganadja, in contrast was a cautious yet curious creature. Rather than sporting with her kind, she preferred to visit the yakuna. They learnt to trust her and taught her about the ways of the ocean, so that she too grew wise and knowledgeable.

Dinginjabana scorned the yakuna because they could not move swiftly through the waves. He became jealous of the time his mate spent with them, and told her to stay away. But Ganadja enjoyed her visits and ignored his warnings. This made him angry. Dinginjabana began to tease the yakuna, swimming up to them fast and swishing his powerful flukes to create a current that sent them spinning over the sand.

Although the yakuna also loved Ganadja, they did not trust the other dolphins. The next time the Indjebena began to tease the yakuna, Baringgwa, the leader of the yakuna, told the dolphins: "All I have to do is shout and Mana, the tiger shark, will come to my rescue."

Large, sleek and with row upon row of sharp teeth, Mana was the dolphins' worst enemy. He would lie quietly on the coral, waiting for an unsuspecting dolphin to swim close, then rush forward slashing and cutting with his teeth until the water ran red with blood. The first time Baringgwa threatened them in this way, all the dolphins forgot their game and swam away, but when they realized the yakuna had not called Mana, they returned to their sporting. Another day, while frisking in and out of the waves, the dolphins once again became tired of their play. Dinginjabana suggested going to find the yakuna. "Let's get Baringgwa and toss him in the air, catching him as he falls back in the water," he cried, and all the other dolphins agreed it would be good fun. Ganadja objected strongly, but her words simply made Dinginjabana more determined and he swam off straight away to look for Baringgwa.

Having found him, Dinginjabana dislodged the yakuna leader from the sand and carried him to the surface. The dolphins then took it in turn to toss Baringgwa into the air, catch him and toss him again—young and old, male and female, all joining in the game. Baringgwa warned them that the yakuna would call the sharks to protect him, but the dolphins laughed. As they played on, black shadows appeared in the deep water beneath the dolphins, who were too pre-occupied to notice. Suddenly, the shadows darted to the surface. As the slaughter began, the sea turned scarlet with dolphin blood. Dinginjabana himself was sliced in half as he tried to swim away. Ganadja, hiding on the yakuna bed, screamed in terror as she saw her husband's head float down next to her. One of the sharks heard her and swam down to find her. Realizing that the shark would certainly find Ganadja, the yakuna cried, "Come press your body right to the bottom. Then we can cover you with our shells!" The shark swam past without noticing her, and Ganadja was saved. She was the only member of the Indjebena tribe to escape the massacre. After several months of desperate loneliness, she gave birth to a fine son which she named Dinginjabana after his father. He grew much larger than the other dolphins, so he did not fear the sight of Mana, the tiger shark. He was the first of the silver tribe of dolphins that we see today.

The souls of the dolphins who were slaughtered became very hard and dry. After much time had passed, they were reborn on dry land, where they became the first human beings. Never again would their spirits swim swiftly through the waves. One night, long after her son had grown up, Ganadja was swimming near the shore when she saw her husband, Dinginjabana, who was now a two-legged man. Thrusting her body up onto the shore, she heaved herself over the sand by her flippers. When Dinginjabana recognized his wife, Ganadja gave a joyful cry and suddenly took the shape of a human being. In time, the human Dinginjabana and Ganadja had many children, who became the people of Groote Island. They are the only ones who remember that dolphins are ancestors of the entire human race. However, all the dolphins swimming in the ocean are the offspring of mother Ganadja, so they have never forgotten that the two-legged people on land are their cousins. This is why, even today, dolphins seek out their human kin to play as they did in the days of the dream-time.

Dolphin Genesis

Susan Lynn Reynolds

In the beginning there was only the sun and the sea. The sun was Raza, Father to all the life that swam in the belly of the Mother. For uncounted ages they existed alone together. But then the spark of a new being appeared beyond the sky, growing closer and larger and more beautiful, until he eclipsed even the beauty of the sun. The newcomer's name was Kryphon and the Mother's being surged toward him. Their meeting was portentous. And then he left her, retreating into the black night once again.

But from their meeting grew new life: a girl and a boy. From deep beneath her, the Mother raised a place where the sea and the sky met for these children to be born, for she knew they would belong both to water and to sky.

In time Calleby and Bedjar were born in this place. They were covered with iridescent scales and breathed

both air and water with equal ease. But unlike any creature ever seen in the world before or since, they also had
legs and arms which streamed away from their bodies as
their father's legs had streamed behind him. When their
ears and eyes opened, the Sea Mother spoke to them in
crashing words: "Look to me and honor me, and as long
as there is beach to stand on, I will care for you."

But Bedjar looked up to the sky, breathed deeply,
and turned his back on the sea. He looked beyond the
beach, found a lactus tree, and climbed its ribbed
trunk. He brought the fruit of the lactus to Calleby and
said, "We need her weaning no more. We walk upon legs
that can climb. We can find our own food and do not
need her gifts."

Calleby, seeing his blue eyes sparkle with the light of
Kryphon, tasted the fruit of the lactus tree.

The Sea Mother shuddered with rage. She slapped
them down with a thundering wall of water and drew
them back into her womb. She stripped them of their
iridescence, the shimmering scales falling from their
bodies like schools of minnows. She smoothed the gills
at their throats and the gills disappeared, leaving no
mark. Finally, she threw them up onto the beach, leaving their soft new skin to bake on the sand.

The Sea Mother called out to all the creatures that
coursed through her, "From this day forth, ignore the

hunger calls of Bedjar and Calleby." The mollusks and conchs and bonitas and krill all turned as one in the sway of her voice and closed their ears forever.

All but doraado, who spoke out, "Oh, Mother-of-all, home-to-all, smoother-of-stones, your punishment is too severe. Calleby is blameless, yet you curse this helpless child because she yielded to Bedjar's eyes, just as you did to Kryphon's light."

The Mother's fury boiled at this reminder of her foolishness. She threw doraado onto the coral and raked the gills from his cheeks and the scales from his back. She flattened his tail and poked a hole in his head so he would be forced always, like Calleby and Bedjar, to take his life from the air.

This is how doraado got his name: dor-a-a-do, "not a fish, not a man," for he could not walk upon the beach or live long in the deepest reaches of the Sea Mother's being.

And this, too, is how doraado became the friend of Calleby of Strandia and all the daughters that came after her.

Apollo Brings Men to Be Priests
An Homeric Hymn to Pythian Apollo

Hesiod

Then Phoebus Apollo pondered in his heart what men he should bring in to be his ministers in sacrifice and to serve him in rocky Pytho [Delphi]. And while he considered this, he became aware of a swift ship upon the wine-like sea in which were many men and goodly, Cretans from Cnossos, the city of Minos. . . . These men were sailing in their black ship for traffic and for profit to sandy Pylos and to the men of Pylos. But Phoebus Apollo met them: in the open sea he sprang upon their swift ship, like a dolphin in shape, and lay there, a great and awesome monster, and none of them gave heed so as to understand; but they sought to cast the dolphin overboard. But he kept shaking the black ship every way and make the timbers quiver. So they sat silent in their craft for fear, and did not loose the sheets throughout the black, hollow ship, nor lowered the sail of their dark-prowed vessel, but as they had set

it first of all with oxhide ropes, so they kept sailing on;
for a rushing south wind hurried on the swift ship from
behind. First they passed by Malea, and then along the
Laconian coast they came to Taenarum, sea-garlanded
town and country of Helios who gladdens men. . . .
There they wished to put their ship to shore, and land
and comprehend the great marvel and see with their
eyes whether the monster [dolphin] would remain
upon the deck of the hollow ship, or spring back into
the briny deep where fishes shoal. But the well-built
ship would not obey the helm, but went on its way all
along Peloponnesus: and the lord, far-working Apollo,
guided it easily with the breath of the breeze. So the
ship ran on its course. . . . The lord Apollo, son of
Zeus, led them on until they reached far-seen Crisa,
land of vines, and into haven: there the sea-coursing
ship grounded on the sands.

Then, like a star at noonday, the lord, far-working
Apollo, leaped from the ship. . . . He entered into his
shrine. . . . From his shrine he sprang forth again, swift
as a thought, to speed again to the ship, bearing the form
of a man, brisk and sturdy, in the prime of his youth,
while his broad shoulders were covered with his hair: and
he spoke to the Cretans, uttering winged words:

"Strangers, who are you? Whence come you sailing
along the paths of the sea?. . ."

So speaking, he put courage in their hearts, and the master of the Cretans answered him and said: "Stranger . . . tell me truly that I may surely know it: what country is this, and what land, and what men live herein? As for us, with thoughts set otherwards, we were sailing over the great sea to Pylos from Crete (for from there we declare that we are sprung), but now are come on shipboard to this place by no means willingly—another way and other paths—and gladly would we return. But one of the deathless gods brought us here against our will."

Then far-working Apollo answered them and said: "Strangers who once dwelt about wooded Cnossos. . . . I am the son of Zeus; Apollo is my name; but you I brought here over the wide gulf of the sea, meaning you no hurt; nay, here you shall keep my rich temple that is greatly honoured among men, and you shall know the plans of the deathless gods, and by their will you shall be honoured continually for all time. . . . [S]tand side by side around the altar and pray: and in as much as at the first on the hazy sea I sprang upon the swift ship in the form of a dolphin, pray to me as Apollo Delphinius; also the altar itself shall be called Delphinius and overlooking forever."

How Dionysus Created Dolphins
An Homeric Hymn to Dionysus

Anonymous

Of him that had for mother the glorious Sémele
I will sing, of Dionysus—how by the barren sea
Upon a jutting headland he stood revealed once, fair
As a stripling in his flower of youth, with raven hair
Tossing about his shoulder, and mantle purple-wove
Round his broad chest. But, swiftly, in sight a tall
    ship hove,
Manned by Tyrsēnian pirates, cleaving beneath her stem
The waste of wine-dark waters—ill hour it was for *them*!
Seeing him they nodded each to each, and speedily
They sprang ashore, and seized him, and dragged with
    savage glee
Aboard their ship. For they deemed him a prince that
    they had caught,
Son of some king by Heaven blest; and bitter gyves they
    brought.
But lo! nothing could hold him—the bonds all slid away

From his hands and feet, and before them, he sat
   there, smiling gay
With eyes of blue. Then the steersman, seeing such
   things befall,
Cried aloud in warning to his comrades one and all:
"Madmen, what God is this that ye seize and bind
   in vain!—
A mightier one is here than *our* ship can contain.
Zeus it must be, or Poseidon, or the Lord of the
   Silver Bow,
Apollo! For only Immortals were ever fashioned so,
That dwell on high Olympus—and none of mortal birth.
Come, let him go in freedom across the dark-loamed
   earth,
Delay no more, unhand him!—for fear that in wrath
   he cast
Some great gale loose against us, some tempest's
   raging blast."
   But angrily the captain made answer: "Keep an eye,
Fool, on the wind behind us, and hoist full sail on high.
This lad is for *men* to handle. If it go as I have planned,
To Cyprus, or to Egypt, or the Hyperborean land—
Or further yet—I will ship him. He shall tell us in
   the end
The names—ay, and the riches—of family and friend,
Seeing that fate was minded to throw him in our way."

With that he hauled at mast and sail; and every stay,
As the breeze swelled out the canvas, they stretched taut
    to the blast.
But suddenly before their eyes strange wonders passed—
First of all, through their swift black ship gushed
    streams of wine,
Sweet to the taste and nostril, while a fragrance all
    divine
Floated around—the seamen stood gaping at the sight.
All up the sail went climbing a vine to left and right,
Loaded with hanging clusters; and high aloft the mast
Dark coils of winding ivy, bright with its flowers,
    clung fast,
All beautiful with berries; and the thole-pin of
    each oar
Stood wreathed with green. To the helmsman, they
    cried to steer for shore;
But, from the prow of the galley, the God's self met
    them there,
Like a grisly lion, with thunderous roar; and a
    shaggy bear,
Rising erect in her fury, by his wonder-working power,
Amidships stood, while forward they saw the lion lour,
Terrible. Then to sternward they huddled, shuddering,
Around the righteous steersman. But, with sudden
    spring,

The lion seized the captain; and the crew, all mad to flee
That evil end, plunged headlong into the sacred sea
And changed at once to dolphins. But, unlike all
    the rest,
The God pitied the helmsman, and held him back, and
    blessed:
"Courage, thou noble heart! I am well pleased with thee.
But *I* am Dionysus, the Lord of Revel—he
Whom Zeus begot on Cadmus' child, His own loved
    Sémele."

Son of fair Sémele, farewell! No man shall raise
Sweet song, save he remember to yield thee too
    thy praise.

The Rescue of Arion

Herodotus

[Arion] had lived for many years at the court of
Periander, when a longing came upon him to sail
across to Italy and Sicily. Having made rich profits in
those parts, he wanted to recross the seas to Corinth.
He therefore hired a vessel, the crew of which were
Corinthians, thinking that there was no people in
whom he could more safely confide; and, going on
board, he set sail from Tarentum. The sailors, however, when they reached the open sea, formed a plot to
throw him overboard and seize upon his riches.
Discovering their design, he fell on his knees,
beseeching them to spare his life, and making them
welcome to his money. But they refused; and required
him either to kill himself outright, if he wished for a
grave on the dry land, or without loss of time to leap
overboard into the sea. In this strait Arion begged
them, since such was their pleasure, to allow him to

mount upon the quarter-deck, dressed in his full costume, and there to play and sing, and promising that, as soon as his song was ended, he would destroy himself. Delighted at the prospect of hearing the very best harper in the world, they consented, and withdrew from the stern to the middle of the vessel: while Arion dressed himself in the full costume of his calling, took his harp, and standing on the quarter-deck, chanted the Orthian. His strain ended, he flung himself, fully attired as he was, headlong into the sea. The Corinthians then sailed on to Corinth. As for Arion, a dolphin, they say, took him upon his back and carried him to Taenarum, where he went ashore, and thence proceeded to Corinth in his musician's dress, and told all that had happened to him. Periander, however, disbelieved the story, and put Arion in ward, to prevent his leaving Corinth, while he watched anxiously for the return of the mariners. On their arrival he summoned them before him and asked them if they could give him any tidings of Arion. They returned for answer that he was alive and in good health in Italy, and that they had left him at Tarentum, where he was doing well. Thereupon Arion appeared before them, just as he was when he jumped from the vessel: the men, astonished and detected in falsehood, could no longer deny their guilt. Such is the account which the

Corinthians and the Lesbians give; and there is to this day at Taenarum, an offering of Arion's at the shrine, which is a small figure in bronze, representing a man seated upon a dolphin.

The Compassion of Dolphins

Aristotle

[A]fter a dolphin had been caught and wounded off the coast of Caria, a shoal of dolphins came into the harbor and stopped there until the fisherman let his captive go free; whereupon the shoal departed. A shoal of young dolphins is always, by way of protection, followed by a [group of] large ones. On one occasion a shoal of dolphins, large and small, was seen, and two dolphins at a little distance appeared swimming in underneath a little dead dolphin when it was sinking, and supporting it on their backs, trying out of compassion to prevent its being devoured by some predacious fish.

On the Intelligence of Animals

Plutarch

Of the land animals, some avoid man altogether, others, the tamest kind, pay court for utilitarian reasons only to those who feed them, as do dogs and horses and elephants to their familiars. Martins take to houses to get what they need, darkness and a minimum of security, but avoid and fear man as a dangerous wild beast. To the dolphin alone, beyond all others, nature has granted what the best philosophers seek: friendship for no advantage. Though it has no need at all of any man, yet it is a genial friend to all and has helped many.

The Dolphin Lover, Part 1
An Amazonian Folktale

retold by Natalia Burns

River dolphins of the Amazon (Inia Geoffrensis) are of course, freshwater dolphins. Clumsier and less intelligent than seagoing dolphins, they have long "beaks" lined with teeth and are almost blind—they are also sometimes bright pink.

None of these factors have stopped them, though, from winning all the honors of their more developed cousins: They are considered sacred and killing or injuring a river dolphin is taboo. As in so many other cultures, people of the Amazon consider the river dolphins to have once been people. The story goes like this: In the time of the gods, one village had a particularly boisterous party. The gods were annoyed and sent heavy rains to quiet them. The rains were so heavy the people began to drown. At the last minute, the gods changed the drowning people into dolphins to save their lives.

One of the most popular stories is the tale of "Bufeo Colorado," the dolphin lover.

Not having learned their lesson about loud parties from the time of the gods, the people of the Amazon still like to have noisy village get-togethers on the banks of the great and ancient river. Everyone comes out to dance, eat mangoes, and make romance. And sometimes an uninvited guest takes advantage of Amazonian hospitality.

Descended from a race of gods who live in the beautiful underwater cities of the Amazon River, "Bufeo Colorado" comes in disguise as a human. Dressed in an immaculate white suit, he looks like a handsome, elegant stranger. But he never takes off his hat—it covers his blowhole, the only part of him not changed in his transformation.

Through the evening he romances the most beautiful woman at the party, dancing only with her into the night. The legend says that if Bufeo Colorado were to take his chosen lady to his home under the waves she would be so enthralled with its beauty and wealth that she wouldn't want to leave. But this time he doesn't take her there. He makes love to her as a man, in her bed, and never tells her his secret. Then he goes back to his beautiful city in the River.

Weeks later, when the woman realizes she's pregnant by the mysterious stranger, she knows she's been seduced by the dolphin lover. And when she registers the birth of her child, she lists the father as—"The Dolphin."

The Dolphin Lover, Part 2
El Encantado

Candace Slater

A second widely held belief regarding Dolphins with a capital "D" [an enchanted dolphin who can turn into a man] concerns their not just fun-loving, but downright lascivious nature. Not only do they dance all night with the prettiest woman at the party, but once the lights and music fade, they show up in her bed. Dona Marina recalls how a handsome young man "white as tapioca" (a pancakelike manioc confection) seduces a young woman despite her father's attempts to shield her from the stranger's advances.

> So then, when the party ended,
>   there around three in the morning,
>   everyone saw that handsome man
>   standing there in the moonlight
>   beneath the banana tree
>   —white as a tapioca, he!

So then, he [the Dolphin] went down toward the
   river.

The girl's father remained there waiting,
   he didn't see anyone pass by.
Because he [the Dolphin] had already gone
   to the man's house!
"That creature is going to end up in my daughter's
   hammock!" the father said when he realized
     what had happened.
So then, he grabbed his harpoon
   and ran home.
But when he arrived on the doorstep,
   the Dolphin was already leaving through the
     window.
There was nothing he could do.

Nine months went by
   and the girl went into labor.
The baby was the image,
   the spitting image of a dolphin!
      —I saw that little dolphin-child with my own
      eyes.

Although Dolphins have a rakish reputation, the
women who become involved with them in these stories

rarely suspect their true identity while they are making love. Only in the morning, when the handsome stranger's shoes turn into stingrays or hard-shelled *bodó* fish, and the hat he has left behind becomes a tortoise that goes ambling off in the direction of the river, do they become aware that something very strange is going on. Occasionally, in the heat of passion, the Dolphin reveals his true identity to the woman, urging her to accompany him to his kingdom beneath the river. . . .

Some Dolphins may appear to the object of their affections not as attractive strangers, but rather, as husbands or lovers. Unlike the partygoers given to one-night stands, these Dolphin impersonators are apt to make repeat appearances in the woman's bed. Usually, the couple realizes that something is amiss when the woman refers to amorous activities in which the man has not engaged. ("Again, Zezinho? But you just left here less than an hour ago! Don't you ever get enough?" The man will then look disconcerted, mumbling something on the order of "But Raimunda, dear, I've been off fishing for three whole days now and I just walked in the door.") . . .

Quite often, the woman herself does not actually see the Dolphin. He arrives when she is already sleeping, or else "hypnotizes" or "magnetizes" her so that she later has no recollection of the encounter. Although the other household members may remark slyly on the hammock's particularly energetic swaying or the woman's drawn-out moans of pleasure, they generally do not suspect what is transpiring. (That is, they do not realize *who* is making the hammock creak.) Often, the Dolphin leaves behind a gift for the object of his affections, most often a ring or necklace, or a silvery pile of fish.

Recurrent visits inevitably have a negative effect upon the still unsuspecting woman, who grows thinner, paler, and more listless with each passing day. ("The woman becomes thin as a fishing pole and yellow, very yellow," Tô Pereira asserts.) Often, her skin will develop a peculiar, soapy texture, and a pronounced fishy smell, and she will display an inexplicable desire to go down to the riverbank at all hours of the day and night. Sometimes, she begins to sing hauntingly lovely songs whose words no one can understand, develops a persistent fever, and reveals incipient signs of madness. If her symptoms are not promptly treated, she either disappears or dies.

Only two hopes exist for the woman who is sleeping with a Dolphin. The first is for a shamanic healer to drive away her tenacious suitor either by direct contact with the offending *encantado* or more indirectly through a strict regimen of ritual baths and defumations. ("The person smells like a walking chili pepper for weeks afterward, but sometimes this is the only hope," Tô Pereira says, pinching his nose.) The only other solution is for one of the woman's family to kill the unwelcome visitor. Sometimes, the woman's husband or lover lies in wait for the Dolphin and harpoons him. On other occasions, the man attacks what he thinks is a human rival, only later to discover his knife embedded in a dolphin.

Dolphins in the Roman Province of Narbonne

Pliny the Elder

In the region of Nismes in the Province of Narbonne there is marsh named Latera where dolphins catch fish in partnership with a human fisherman. At a regular season a countless shoal of mullet rushes out of the narrow mouth of the marsh into the sea, after watching for the turn of the tide, which makes it impossible for nets to be spread across the channel—indeed the nets would be equally incapable of standing the mass of the weight even if the craft of the fish did not watch for the opportunity. For a similar reason they make straight out into the deep water produced by the neighbouring eddies, and hasten to escape from the only place suitable for setting nets. When this is observed by the fishermen—and a crowd collects at the place, as they know the time, and even more because of their keenness for this sport—and when the entire population from the shore shouts as loud as it can, calling for 'Snub-nose' for the dénouement of the show, the dolphins quickly hear their wishes if a northerly breeze carries the shout out to sea, though if the wind is in the south, against the sound, it carries it more slowly; but then too they suddenly hasten to the spot, in order to give their aid. Their line of battle comes into view, and at once deploys in the place where they are to join battle; they bar the passage on the side of the sea and drive the scared mullet into the shallows. Then the fishermen put their nets round them and lift them out of the water with forks. None the less the pace of some mullets leaps over the obstacles; but these are caught by the dolphins, which are satisfied for the time being with merely having killed them, postponing a meal till victory is won. The action is hotly contested, and the dolphins pressing on with the greatest bravery are delighted to be caught in the nets, and for fear that this itself may hasten the enemy's flight, they glide out between the boats and the nets or the swimming fishermen so gradually as not to open ways of escape; none of them try to get away by leaping out of the water, which otherwise they are very fond of doing, unless the nets are put below them. One that gets out thereupon carries on the battle in front of the rampart. When in this way the catch has been completed they tear in pieces the fish that they have killed. But as they are aware that they have had too strenuous a task for only a single day's pay they wait there till the following day, and are given a feed of bread mash dipped in wine, in addition to the fish.

Mucianus's account of the same kind of fishing in the Iasian Gulf differs in this—the dolphins stand by of their own accord and without being summoned by a shout, and receive their share from the fishermen's hands, and each boat has one of the dolphins as its ally although it is in the night and by torchlight. The dolphins also have a form of public alliance of their own: when one was caught by the King of Caria and kept tied up in the harbour a great multitude of the remainder assembled, suing for compassion with an unmistakable display of grief, until the king ordered it to be released. Moreover small dolphins are always accompanied by a larger one as escort; and before now dolphins have been seen carrying a dead comrade, to prevent its body being torn in pieces by sea-monsters.

How the Heir to the French Throne Came to Be Called "The Dolphin"

A Speculation

Katharine K. Wiley

"Le Dauphin" is a French aristocratic title that literally means "The Dolphin." It originally was reserved for the counts of Vienne, then, after 1349 and until 1830, the eldest son of the King of France. If the eldest son died before the king died then the title went to the Dauphin's son.

The royal family acquired the title, along with a coat of arms featuring three dolphins, when Charles of Valois, the future Charles the Fifth, bought an area called Le Dauphine, or the Place of the Dolphins. The Dauphine happens to correspond to the old Roman province of Narbonne in the southeast of France, from roughly the Côte D'Azur to Narbonne, with Nimes in the middle, where Pliny the Elder described dolphins helping locals fish. It's possible that Le Dauphine got its name, and associated honors, from those ancient days when dolphins fished with men in France.

Dolphins in the Desert

Nelson Glueck

In any kind of fashion show for goddesses of the ancient Near East, the Atargatis of Khirbet Tannur would easily have won the prize as the best dressed one of them all. She had a different and striking costume for apparently every conceivable occasion, with changes for every day of the week and more. . . .

In one costume she appeared as the Grain Goddess and in the other as the Dolphin Goddess, with the latter being the most unusual of them all. On the small top of a steep-sided hill, in a canyon-split land edged on several sides by immense deserts and bordered on another by a wild, deep, practically waterless rift difficult of access, in an isolated sanctuary many weary miles removed from any sea and its creatures, this Atargatis of Tannur wore a headdress of dolphins! . . .

Meeting her, as we did, practically in the middle of the desert, flaunting dolphins on top of her head, seemed at first almost as strange as it would have been to have encountered a camel swimming far out at sea. It took considerable scientific detective work to ascertain that the ornament of dolphins was as highly esteemed by the Nabataeans as were the symbols of fruit or foliage or grain and that worship of the dolphin Goddess was held to be as important for travel by land as for voyage by sea. Indeed, especial reverence was accorded dolphins for the help they were supposed to be able to give on the journey that every one sooner or later had to undertake into the blue beyond of life after death. . . .

Where then did the Dolphin Goddess of Khirbet Tannur come from? With what juncture of events and impacts is she to be connected? She was no Athena sprung full-grown from Zeus's head. An innumerable series of overlapping circles of political and cultural and religious conditions and circumstances were intertwined in her coming into being and occupying a place of central symbolic prominence in the family of deities to which the Nabataeans and countless others paid glad homage. . . .

Was it because of the nearness and wonder of drinkable water in the midst of the desert that the widely traveled Nabataean caravaneers, trafficking between the Persian Gulf and the Red and Mediterranean Seas, introduced the images of dolphins into

the fabric of their worship? That hardly seems suffi-
cient reason. Or was it because of a very direct connection that had been established between dolphins and
travel as such whether by sea or land, whether in this
life or beyond it?

Why a dolphin altar at Abda in the desert of the
Negev, which depended upon waters painfully garnered
through unbelievably extensive and intricate devices
from the desert's brief season rains? Why sculptures of
dolphins in the deep clefts of the earth's crust that
marked the location of Petra, as hidden as could be
from the sound and smell and roll and fury of the sea?
Why the reliefs of dolphins on the head of Atargatis at
the mountaintop temple of Khirbet Tannur, that used
cistern water for immediate purposes? The permanent
stream at the bottom of the deep canyon of the Wadi
Hesa (River Zered) below it to the north was a good
hour's walking distance away and more down and back
again in each direction.

It would seem then that it was neither the nearness
nor the remoteness of living waters either in the compara-
tively fertile highlands or in the unrelievedly sere deserts
of the Nabataean kingdom that determined the presence
of dolphin sculptures in Nabataean temples. . . .

It is evident, therefore, that the frame of reference
in which the Nabataean and Parthian dolphins and

other sea creatures are contained must be widened to include Hellenistic places as distant from Khirbet Tannur and Petra and Hatra as Aphrodisias and Olbia and Kerch. The latter two places especially and others of the same type, a few of which we have mentioned, must have been frequented also by Scythians as well as by Greek colonists and traders. . . . There is little doubt, however, that the most immediate background of the use of the dolphin by the Nabataeans is Greek. The purpose of placing dolphin tokens in the hands of the dead seems to have been to assure a safe voyage for those who had to traverse the uncharted regions of after-life.

Halieutica

Oppian

The hunting of Dolphins is immoral and that man can no more draw nigh the gods as a welcome sacrificer nor touch their altars with clean hands but pollutes those who share the same roof with him, whoso willingly devises destruction for Dolphins. For equally with human slaughter the gods abhor the deathly doom of the monarchs of the deep.

The White Goddess of the Yellow River

Zhou Kaiya and Zhang Xingduan

Once upon a time there was on the south bank a beautiful and kind-hearted girl who had lost her father and was living with her stepfather. She was maltreated and often savagely beaten. One day the stepfather found, to his surprise, that she had grown into a slim and graceful maiden. He hit upon a sinister idea. He coaxed the girl to get aboard a hired boat in an attempt to sell her for a fortune to a trader in women on the north bank.

Halfway in the river, they were caught in a downpour and were soaked through. Her ivory-like body, graceful figure and firm breasts were half visible behind her thin wet dress. At the sight, the old brute became fascinated and felt a rush of fire in his loins. He grabbed her into his arms, dragged her into the cabin and was about to violate her there and then. The girl realized what was happening and was struck with horror. She knew she had been cheated. He intended not only to rape her but also sell her after that. An even more miserable fate awaited her. She broke free, dashed out into the driving wind and blinding rain, and plunged into the river.

Instantly wind howled and waves surged, capsizing the boat. The vicious man struggled for a while and was whirled down to the bottom.

The storm stopped as abruptly as it had broken out. People on both banks saw a slim and beautiful baiji swimming and playing freely in the river. "That's the incarnation of the beautiful girl," so everybody said. Seen frequently in her wake was a short, ugly black finless porpoise, which was believed to be the shameless stepfather incarnate, and which people call a "river pig." God was full of sympathy for the unfortunate girl and made her a goddess in charge of ships and boats sailing in the Yangtze. The stepfather was condemned to be a "river pig" forever.

The Story of Bai Qiulian

Zhou Kaiya and Zhang Xingduan

Of all the legends concerning baiji, the most fantastic and moving is the story of Bai Qiulian from *Strange Tales of Liaozhai*, a collection of mythical short stories by the outstanding 17th-century Chinese writer Pu Songling. In the story the author portrays the baiji as goddess of the Yangtze, kind and beautiful, graceful and passionate.

Musheng, son of a merchant in Peking, had an ardent love for poetry since childhood. At the age of sixteen he traveled with his father to Wuchang (present-day Wuhan, Hubei Province) in the middle reaches of the Yangtze to do business there. His father went into the city while Musheng stayed behind in their boat, studying classical poetry. One night he was absorbed in his studies, reading aloud in a melodious and sonorous tone, when he saw a human figure flash past his window. He paid no attention at first. But when the moon had risen, he clearly saw the silhouette of a female lingering outside his window. He rushed out to find a charming young girl, who shyly fled at the sight of him.

Three days later, their boat was loaded with goods that his father had purchased, and they were about to set sail on their return trip. Night came and his father went ashore. An old woman rushed onto his boat and said to him, "My daughter is dying because of you!" Musheng was puzzled. She then said that her youngest daughter Bai Qiulian had heard him recite a poem at Wuchang and lost her heart to him. She had refused food and drink the last three days and was very weak now. The mother had come to implore him to marry her daughter Qiulian.

Musheng loved the girl, but he hesitated for fear that his father might not give his consent. The old woman grew furious and said, "You'll never want to get to Peking if you are so unreasonable!"

Early the next morning they set sail. But all of a sudden a sandbar surged up from underwater where their boat lay at anchor. They were stranded. His father could only go back to Peking by land, leaving Musheng behind to look after the goods. He was delighted and went around asking about the where-abouts of Bai Qiulian.

Night came and he was sitting alone in his cabin distressed. There came the sound of footsteps. The old

woman reappeared, leading her daughter by the hand—
the very girl he had seen outside his window. Musheng
was deeply touched to see Qiulian so very ill. However,
Bai Qiulian said, "I'll recover when I've heard you
recite the poem you did that night."

Musheng did as he was asked.

"I've been tossing about in bed,
Reluctant to rise,
Since I became emaciated
And my face lost its radiance.
Not bashful that others think me lazy,
I'm afraid, my sweetheart,
You should see me so haggard
For I miss you day and night."

No sooner had Musheng finished reciting the
poem for a third time than the girl sprang to her feet
and joined him in the recitation. That night, after
the old woman left, they plunged into each other's
passionate arms.

Months went by and the spring flood came.
Musheng's father returned. He was annoyed and repri-
manded his son on learning that he had fallen in love
with a girl. Later, however he softened when he saw the
sad and sickly look on his son's face and allowed Bai

Qiulian to stay aboard their boat to keep his son company. She was not only a good-natured charming girl, but also helped in their business, thus giving Musheng's father a favorable impression. Musheng and Bai Qiulian got married and decided to go back to Peking together. She brought with her a jar of water scooped from the Dongting Lake and would add a little bit of the water every time she did the cooking to make the food delicious.

Three or four years later, Bai Qiulian gave birth to a son. One day she longed for home and said, tears in her eyes, that she wanted to go back to the Dongting. So the couple came down with their baby son in a merchant ship. When night came, she would knock at the side of the ship and call out her mother's name. She sent her husband everywhere around the lake inquiring about her mother, but she was nowhere to be found.

One day a fisherman caught a huge fish resembling a human being with breasts and female organs. The local people called this fish baiji. Qiulian was taken aback by the news and begged her husband to buy the captured creature for whatever price was asked and free the captive animal. Musheng did as he was asked. To his surprise, the moment he let go of the animal, Bai Qiulian also disappeared and did not return until the following day.

Only then did Bai Qiulian tell her husband all the truth about herself and her mother. The baiji that Musheng had bought and set free was none other than her mother. Previously she and her mother had dwelled in the Dongting Lake, entrusted by the Dragon King with boats and ships sailing there. Somehow the Dragon King had heard about the extraordinary beauty of Bai Qiulian and wanted to make her his imperial concubine, demanding that her mother bring her to his palace at once. He flew into a rage after she told him that her daughter had been married and had a son, and gave the decree that she be banished onto a sandbar of the lake. She was dying of hunger when a fisherman caught her. Though now she had been set free, the Dragon King was not likely to stop at that. She paused and, straightening her dress, continued, "If you dislike me just because I'm not a human being, then take your son with you and I'll go back to the Dragon King's imperial palace. Life there is a hundred times better than in the human world. If you do love me and want us to remain a devoted couple to the end of our lives, you must do one thing to save my mother."

Musheng was deeply touched by her honesty and her love for him. He went to a lame Taoist priest in a dilapidated temple as his wife told him. He went down on his knees in front of the priest and told him everything about their devotion and love. The priest said with a smile, "Indeed, this baiji is exceptionally noble and charming. She prefers an ordinary mortal like you to the riches and splendor in the Dragon King's palace. The old dragon shall never be allowed to go so loose and unashamed!" Having said this, he wrote on a piece of white silk the Chinese character EXEMPTED and gave it to Musheng. The priest turned out to be a divine being.

Bai Qiulian and her mother were saved. Musheng and Qiulian remained an affectionate couple, living happily on the lakeside with their sons and daughters. They favored the people around the Dongting and along the Yangtze, warning them of forthcoming wind and rain, awarding the good and punishing the evil.

A Song in Praise of the "Goddess of the Yangtze"

Zhou Kaiya and Zhang Xingduan

Fishermen and boatmen in areas round the Dongting Lake and in the middle reaches of the Yangtze have all along regarded the baiji as their goddess of protection. Whenever there was going to be a storm, a shoal of baiji would come forth swimming and leaping swiftly. They believed their appearance to be a message from their "Goddess of the Yangtze"—a warning to them that they must lie at anchor.

They were convinced that those who had done anything evil would not be able to see the goddess, and that whoever captured or hurt a baiji would never escape a tragic end.

Following is a poem of China's Song Dynasty giving a vivid account of how fishermen and boatmen are protected from a forthcoming storm by their goddess:

Calm and tranquil is the Yangtze,
Ten thousand li [five thousand kilometers] of glittering ripples.
Baiji are coming, emerging in pairs,
Their beaklike snouts above water.
Now diving and leaping,
Now playing and chasing.
Alarmed are the boatmen, aware
A storm is approaching.
They hurry back to the harbor and
Moor their boats with hawsers.
Sure enough, there blow gusts of wind
With mountainous waves dashing and howling;
The world is enveloped in mist and clouds.
Safe and sound, the boatmen stay in the harbor
As though in a heavily guarded fortress.
Ah, thank you, Goddess Baiji,
You've saved us from a disaster,
And we'll always remember your favors.

The Milkmaid and the Priest
A Story from Pakistan about
the Indus River Dolphin

retold by Gill Braulik

Once a milkmaid was late in supplying a pir (a priest) who was greatly offended at the delay. He pushed her into the river and said, "You will say push, push all the time." Since then, according to the local folklore the dolphin woman roams the river uttering the "push, push" sound.

Dolphins in Christian Art

George Ferguson

The dolphin is portrayed in Christian art more frequently than any other fish. Generally, it has come to symbolize resurrection and salvation. Considered to be the strongest and swiftest of the fishes, it was often shown bearing the souls of the dead across the waters to the world beyond. Depicted with an anchor or a boat, it symbolized the Christian soul, or the Church, being guided toward salvation by Christ. It frequently represented the whale in the story of Jonah. This, in turn, led to the use of the dolphin as a symbol of the Resurrection and also, though more rarely, as a symbol of Christ.

The Dolphin as Symbol

J. E. Cirlot

The figure of the dolphin can be seen in many allegories and emblems, sometimes duplicated. When the two dolphins—or even figures representing an indeterminate fish—are pointing in the same direction, the duplication may be obeying the dictates of the law of bilateral symmetry for merely ornamental reasons, or it may be a simple symbol of equipoise. But the inverted arrangement, that is, with one dolphin pointing upwards and the other downwards, always symbolizes the dual cosmic streams of involution and evolution; this is what the 17th-century Spanish writer Saavedra Fajardo meant by "Either up or down." The dolphin by itself is an allegory of salvation, inspired in the ancient legends which show it as the friend of man. Its figure is associated with that of the anchor (another symbol of salvation), with pagan, erotic deities and with other symbols. The ancients also held that the dolphin was the swiftest of marine animals, and hence, when, among the emblems of Francesco Colonna, it is shown twined round an anchor, it comes to signify arrested speed, that is, prudence.

Galileo and the Dolphins

Adrian Berry

[T]he most extraordinary dolphin story concerns not their behaviour but politics and the history of science. It tells how a dolphin—or rather the emblem of one— is believed to have been responsible for the trial of Galileo.

This theory, propounded in the *Scientific American* of November 1986 and increasingly accepted by scientific historians, turns on a fact that has hitherto been barely credible—that a harmless 70-year-old man should have been threatened with torture and the stake merely for saying that Jupiter had moons and that the Earth orbits the Sun.

It is said that the inquisitors, obsessed with the printer's emblem of three dolphins on the title page of his *Dialogue of the Two Chief World Systems*, became convinced that Galileo was a Protestant political agent. The year was 1632. The Thirty Years War was raging and there was a paranoid feeling among Catholic religious bureau-crats who were addicted to narrow scholasticism.

Dolphins? The very name might have been calcu-lated to enrage them. Dolphins were associated with the shrine of the god Apollo at Delphi. In Homer's *Iliad*, Apollo was the chief divine supporter of the Trojans. One of the Trojan survivors, Francus, was the legendary founder of the French royal house. "Dolphin" also meant "dauphin," the heir to the French throne. France, at this time, was supporting the Protestant cause. Hence, to a Catholic, the image of a dolphin was treasonable.

We may find dolphins fascinating. In the end, Galileo's feelings are likely to have been more mixed.

Dickens and the Dolphins

Charles Dickens

When all these means of entertainment failed, a sail would heave in sight; looming, perhaps, the very spirit of a ship, in the misty distance, or passing us so close that through our glasses we could see the people on her decks, and easily make out her name, and whither she was bound. For hours together we could watch the dolphins and porpoises as they rolled and leaped and dived around the vessel; or those small creatures ever on the wing, the Mother Carey's chickens, which had borne us company from New York bay, and for a whole fortnight fluttered about the vessel's stern. For some days we had a dead calm, or very light winds, during which the crew amused themselves with fishing, and hooked an unlucky dolphin, who expired, in all his rainbow colours, on the deck: an event of such importance in our barren calendar, that afterwards we dated from the dolphin, and made the day on which he died, an era.

Whales Weep Not!

D. H. Lawrence

. . . and Venus among the fishes skips and is a
    she-dolphin
she is the gay, delighted porpoise sporting with love
    and the sea
she is the female tunny-fish, round and happy among
    the males
and dense with happy blood, dark rainbow bliss in
    the sea.

Part Two

Dolphin Dance

In modern times we've grown apart from our water-world cousins. Our meetings are rarer and more tentative; we've become strangers, even antagonists, although the ancient tingle of connectedness is still present. But if we've forgotten our ancient bond, the dolphins haven't. Shyer now, they still seek to bridge our two worlds. These stories tell of dolphins rescuing us, their clumsy cousins still encumbered with two legs; helping us fish; and inspiring us with their physical beauty.

And whenever we can, we return the favor.

The Fisherman's Porpoise

F. Bruce Lamb

My most interesting experience with a porpoise
occurred near the village of São Luiz, our temporary
operating base for PBY flying boats below the first
rapids on the Tapajós [a tributary of the Amazon
River]. We arrived by launch several days before the
scheduled monthly arrival of the flying boat to prepare
for flights to isolated rubber camps in the wilds of
Mato Grosso. My Brazilian mechanic struck up a
friendship with the local jack-of-all-trades—
mechanic, blacksmith, gunsmith—a young fellow
named Rymundo Mucuim (Raymond Chigger). One
evening just at nightfall we saw Rymundo leaving the
boat landing, where we were tied up, with his canoe
filled with fishing gear. About midnight he returned
with a good catch and left us some fish for our lunch
next day. Later, when he was on board talking shop
with my mechanic, I expressed interest in going fishing

with him sometime. He agreed to pick me up the next good night for fishing.

A few evenings later as the waning moon was going down in the west, Rymundo and a companion paddled up in a canoe to take me fishing. Effortlessly, we floated down river with the current in the still, tropical dusk. There was a faint reflection of moonlight on the water as the soft evening breeze turned up small ripples. In the background the roar of the rapids gradually died away and night sounds of the jungle began to reach us as we moved downstream away from village and rapids. The chirping of tree frogs, the plaintive whistling call of the tree sloth, and an occasional deep-throated grunt of a bull alligator added to the atmosphere of the tropical night.

Rymundo prolonged my anticipation for the fishing by stopping off at Villa Braga, a small trading post, to see his current sweetheart—using the excuse that it was still too light for good fishing. While the young couple carried on their affair, I listened with great interest to an old timer who was full of tales about the early days on the river, tales of previous rubber booms and of the Cuiabanos who came down the Tapajós from the gold and diamond fields of Mato Grosso to trade gold dust for food and supplies, before routes were opened up to south Brazil.

Finally, social affairs concluded, we found our way back in darkness to the canoe and shoved off once more on our way to the fishing grounds. Rymundo busied himself in the bow with his lamp and harpoons, while the other man guided our progress downstream.

My curiosity was aroused by the paddler, who began tapping on the side of the canoe with his paddle between strokes and whistling a peculiar call. Asking Rymundo about this, he startled me by casually remarking that they were calling their *boto*, their porpoise. This struck me as the purest nonsense, especially after the tales I had heard about porpoises spoiling the fishing. However, Rymundo assured me that he had a certain porpoise trained to come when he called and to help him fish. After two years in the Amazon jungles I had learned to keep an open mind toward the unbelievable, so I sat silently waiting.

As we approached the fishing grounds near the riverbank, Rymundo lit his carbide miner's light, adjusted the reflector, chose his first harpoon, and stood up in the bow, ready for action. Almost immediately on the offshore side of the canoe about 50 feet from us we heard the porpoise come up to blow and take in fresh air. "Now we're all set," remarked Rymundo, "everybody's here and ready to go."

Directions were given to the paddler, and we moved in among some rocks in quiet shallow water near shore. Rymundo, his harpoon poised above his head, turned his light to illuminate the river bottom. There came a quick thrust followed by the violent vibration of the harpoon handle, which rose out of the water. A grotesque, dark brown fish was soon brought thrashing out of the water into the canoe. Rymundo had some difficulty withdrawing his harpoon from the hard leathery skin of the fish, and I noticed he was very careful not to touch the fish with his hands. "He has dangerous spines," remarked the fisherman, "but he's much better to eat than his looks indicate!"

As we progressed, the fish scattered ahead of us and went for deep water, but there they encountered our friend the porpoise, who was also fishing, and so they came rushing back to the shallows. Several times they sped back so fast they ended up flopping on the beach. At regular intervals of a few minutes, we could hear our fishing companion come up for a breath of fresh air, and occasionally a ray of light would gleam off his shiny body as he rose partly out of the water just off our deepwater side. . . .

Many strange fish were brought into the canoe as the fishing progressed, and the *boto* stayed right with us as we moved downstream. Finally this section of the fishing grounds had been completely covered, but Rymundo found his catch still insufficient for his steady customers, so he decided to cross the river to another area. Both men took up paddles, and off we went. Failing to hear the porpoise blow for quite a while, I asked about him. The men told me the *boto* lacked patience for such slow travel (it took us about fifteen minutes to cross the river) but he would be waiting when we arrived at the new fishing grounds.

This was no exaggeration, for when we resumed fishing, there he was offshore, giving us his full support and no doubt getting just as good a catch as we were. Returning to São Luiz about midnight, the fishermen assured me that this same porpoise helped them in all their night fishing, scaring the fish from the deep water back to the shallows just as the fishermen scared them out to the porpoise. There seemed little doubt that Rymundo's fishing benefited by the action of friend *boto*. Although some scientists may not agree that wild animals can be induced to co-operate with man in the manner indicated by this experience, I would urge them to await further checking by other careful observers. The porpoise actually accompanied us at 50 to 100 feet for over an hour. This differed greatly from the random feeding movements I have seen porpoises engage in on other occasions.

. . . There was never another opportunity to go fishing with Raymond Chigger, but I have no doubt that he and his porpoise continued by their co-operative effort to provide food for the river village of São Luiz on the Tapajós.

Saved by a Porpoise

Anonymous

We had at the time a narrow beach, reached by a flight of slippery and a bit rickety steps. When I went out to my cabana, no one was in sight, nor did anyone appear when I went swimming, although my husband had asked the owner to keep his eye on me while he was away.

The waves were not over two feet high, and I waded out just waist deep before I realized that there was a terrific undertow. Just as I started to turn back, the undertow swept my feet from under me and knocked me flat in the water. I swallowed a lot of water and, in spite of repeated tries, could not get my footing. I tried to call, but between the water in my lungs and my real fright, I suppose my voice was not loud enough. I realized that, while only about ten feet from shore, there was no way I could make it, and I kept thinking, as I gradually lost consciousness, please God can't someone push me ashore.

With that, someone gave me a tremendous shove, and I landed on the beach, face down, too exhausted to turn over. I kept thinking that I must turn over and thank the person who helped me. It was several minutes before I could do so, and when I did, no one was near, but in the water about eighteen feet out a porpoise was leaping around, and a few feet beyond him another large fish was also leaping.

When I got enough energy to get back up the steps, a man who had been standing on the other side of the fence on the public beach came running over. He asked me how I was and said that he had seen only the last part. It was the second time, he asserted, that he had seen such a thing happen. He said that when he had arrived, I looked like a dead body and that the porpoise shoved me ashore. It was his belief that the porpoise was trying to protect me from the other fish, which he described as a fishtail shark. God certainly was with me.

Rescue off the Bahamas

Yvonne M. Bliss

After floating, swimming, shedding more clothing for what seemed to be an eternity, I saw a form in the water to the left of me. I thought it might be my jacket following along with the tide. Taking a better look I realized it was not the jacket, but some sort of sea life. It touched the side of my hip and thinking it must be a shark, I moved over to the right to try to get away from it. It took a great deal of concentration to keep from panicking. This change in position was to my advantage as heretofore I was bucking a cross tide and the waves would wash over my head and I would swallow a great deal of water. This sea animal which I knew by this time must be a porpoise had guided me so that I was being carried with the tide.

After another eternity and being thankful that my friend was keeping away the sharks and barracuda for which these waters are famous, the porpoise moved back of me and came around to my right side. I moved over to give room to my companion and later knew that had not the porpoise done this, I would have been going down stream to deeper and faster moving waters. The porpoise had guided me to the section where the water was the most shallow.

Shortly I touched what felt like fish netting to my feet. It was seaweed and under that the glorious and most welcome bottom.

As I turned toward shore, stumbling, losing balance and saying a prayer of thanks, my rescuer took off like a streak on down the channel.

A Maori Belief

Frank Robson

"When my husband went out with Frank and Bruce that night, I put a blessing on them. I stood on the beach and put a blessing on them. They didn't know it but I did.

"I knew those fellows wouldn't hurt a dolphin but there were other boats and divers out there and I didn't know if all those people could be trusted. They might do something bad to the dolphin and I didn't want our boys mixed up in anything bad that might happen then.

"Me, I have mixed feelings about that dolphin. A dolphin is a sign—a tohu. But a sign of what? I don't know yet whether this one is a good or a bad sign. I suppose it depends on the people and what they make of it.

"I heard about the dolphin from my husband. He came home from fishing. He was cleaning his gear. He said, 'We've got a mate out there, a dolphin. He keeps nosing around and diving and playing with us.'

"I said, 'How do feel about it? Have you got any funny feelings about it?'

'No. Why should I?'

'You know a dolphin is a tohu, a sign?'

'A sign of what? You tell me that.'

'I couldn't tell him. I didn't know.'

"But I do know that Maoris have a special affinity with dolphins. Maoris are fishermen and dolphins are friends of fishermen. My old ones and my own father have all been fishermen. If they were out in a boat and they saw a dolphin they always treated it with respect. They never took a dolphin for granted just like anything else that swims in the sea. They knew it was a sign of the protection of their ancestors. They knew it was a tohu.

"I knew a man up north. He was diving for kinas (sea-eggs) commercially. He came in from one of the islands and sat down to eat with us. He said he'd been coming in his boat and he saw dolphins alongside. He got one. I couldn't believe what he was saying.

'Don't tell me you speared it?' He nodded.

'I did. And I pulled it alongside my boat.'

'Didn't you know better than that? Didn't your elders tell you about dolphins.'

'No.'

'They didn't tell you that we have to look after them because they look after us?'

'No. I never heard that. We lived in the bush most of our lives. We didn't know much about the sea then.'

"I said, 'Just the same, your old ones should have taught you properly and not let you grow up ignorant about these things. You've done a terrible thing.'

"A few days later he was coming in again in his boat. He was coming over the river bar. Everything was perfectly calm. Then his boat just overturned and he lost all his gear and his food and everything in the boat. He was lucky that was all he lost.

"I asked my husband again, 'Have you thought about your feelings towards that dolphin?'

"He said, 'Look, I'm just glad we've got a mate out there.'

'All right then,' I said. 'You just see that no one does anything to that dolphin. You tell them all that it isn't safe to mess around with that dolphin.'"

Comrade Dolphin

United Press International

MOSCOW—A dolphin set free by Soviet fishermen after it had become entangled in their nets led the fishermen to large shoals of herring, apparently out of gratitude, it was reported here recently.

The Tass press agency said that when the dolphin was set free, it swam ahead of the trawler in the North Sea and then began to circle around the ship, leaping out of the water before the bow. "The navigator had a brainwave and switched on the echo sounder, which indicated a large school of fish," Tass said.

The dolphin returned to the ship each day and the trawler's hold was filled with twice again as many fish as called for in its official quota.

A month later, when the fishermen returned to the same spot, the dolphin met them again and the dolphin-trawler rendezvous continued for four expeditions.

The fifth time, the dolphin was late by a day, Tass said. "He was swimming slowly, and there was a gaping wound in his right side, apparently inflicted by a shark."

The wounded dolphin led the trawler to a herring shoal, then disappeared and was never seen again.

Boy on a Dolphin

Horace Dobbs

I had another twelve hours on the Isle of Man. I stopped packing immediately and announced to Maura and Ashley that we had time to pay Donald another visit before we departed.

It was an opportunity I could not miss, and I took my 16-mm movie camera into the water to film the dolphin we had all come to love.

Donald appeared so quickly I got the impression he had been waiting for us. I framed him up in the viewfinder and pressed the shutter release. As soon as the camera motor started to whir Donald came straight for me, and pushed his snout onto the front of the camera housing. I stopped filming and tried to push him away, but as he was much larger I succeeded only in pushing myself backward.

When he had fully satisfied his curiosity he swam off to inspect Ashley, who was snorkeling down to take the dolphin's photograph with one of my still cameras.

Ashley's antics then set Donald into a frenzy of excitement. From below I could see showers of bubbles as the dolphin leapt clear of the water and splashed in again within inches of my son. I continued filming from underneath, but when I saw the dolphin make a headlong rush for Ashley I feared that Donald's exuberance might override his gentle nature, and I hastened to the surface to tell Ashley to get into the dinghy. As I surfaced I saw a sight that is now etched on my memory.

Ashley rose gently out of the water.

At first his expression was one of incredulity and slight apprehension. Then when he realized what was happening he relaxed. He looked in my direction. His snorkel mouthpiece dropped from his lips and he gave me a broad grin. As he did so he held both of his hands in the air while sitting perfectly balanced on the head of the dolphin. Donald accelerated away from me with Ashley riding, legs astride Donald's head. The dolphin gradually increased speed until he was moving at an impressive rate. He took the course of an arc that swept round the harbor and then brought Ashley back to near where he had started.

Then the dolphin sounded, leaving Ashley to sink slowly in the water again like a water skier who has released the tow rope after a run.

That beautiful and spontaneous act—Ashley said afterward that it came as a complete surprise to him— left me with a joy which even now I cannot adequately describe. The power and simultaneous gentleness with which the dolphin lifted Ashley so smoothly and held him as safely as if he had been on a barber's chair forged a bond between Donald and me as strong and tender as the trust between lovers.

The Dolphin Grandmother

Frank Robson

A party of five Aborigines arrived on location. Bob had recently come to know about this tribe who lived way up in the Northern Territory. They were called the Dolphin People because of a sacred legend in their tribe. The film company chartered a plane and flew them to Monkey Mia from their northern home. It was found then that they could only stay one night. Just before they left a member of their tribe had died and, since they were all people of some standing in their tribe, it was essential that they should be with their people at that time. There were four headmen and their leader who was called Alex.

Every year this tribe holds two ceremonies in honour of the dolphin legend. The first ritual may be attended by all members of the tribe but the other is of a more sacred nature. It may only be witnessed by males and, even then, by men past the age of adolescence.

What takes place at this ceremony is a secret closely guarded from the young people and the women of the tribe. Alex is the master of ceremonies at these rituals. He is known as the Dolphin Grandmother and is the main source of knowledge about the legend. There is no written information on this matter and it is his task to see it handed on to another generation. It was quite clear to me that Alex, the Grandmother of the legend, would make his own decision about how much was to be disclosed in this TV situation, although he made it clear through the interpreter that he was prepared to give some information.

Because their stay was to be so brief, the film crew lost no time in filming the sequences for which the Aborigines had been engaged. With cameras and soundmen all around us, the Aborigines and I were directed to walk down to the water to the dolphins. The idea was to capture the reaction of the Aborigines to the meeting. They were overwhelmed. Everyone was surprised since their tribal identity is based on the dolphin. I got a mental flash from them at once and burst out with what I saw.

"They've never seen a dolphin at close range before," I said.

"How do you know that?"

"I know it. Ask the interpreter."

By this time the men were in the water with the dolphins. They patted them and stroked them and jabbered away in their own language. The director asked the interpreter to ask them if they had ever been so close to a dolphin before. Their reply was clear: they had not.

They stood in the water and waved their arms to the horizon. I knew that they were saying they had only seen them way out on the sea. I was beginning to realise with great excitement that this ancient people might have retained intact the ability for non-verbal communication.

Alex's big scene was the one in which he would explain the background of the dolphin legend. He was positioned facing me with a background of his companions behind him. The cameras whirred as Alex spoke to me. His combination of fast speech and quick hand gestures conveyed not a thing to anyone but before he had finished speaking I had in my mind the picture he was trying to convey.

Bob, the director, gave his impression of what Alex had said. I disagreed with him and he asked for my version. With the picture I had received from Alex still in my mind, I related what I took from it. I saw the expression on Alex's face that he was receiving back the picture he had given.

Bob turned to the interpreter for confirmation and was told that I had more or less repeated what Alex had said. The mental image I received from Alex told this story:

> Long ago, in the area where his ancestor lived, there was a large island but it had no springs of fresh water and was therefore uninhabitable. One day a large shark pursued a dolphin into the inshore waters of this island and finally bit it in two. So great was the speed of the chase that the front part of the dolphin, which was out of the water and in the air in its attempt to evade the snapping jaws, flew on through the air and landed with terrific force on the island. A large crater was caused by the impact and this began to fill with water from an underground spring. The island was then habitable and has been the home of the tribe since that day.

Someone asked what happened to the tail end of the dolphin. Did the shark eat it? There was some animated talk and it was clear that the answer was no. I was able to tell them what Alex was saying as I got the picture plainly in my mind as he spoke. The distinctive shape of the tail-end of the dolphin, flukes and all, can still be seen in the face off the sea-cliff on the island. From this time on, I felt I was accepted by the men as one of themselves—to a certain degree.

How the legend is commemorated in the secret rituals is anyone's guess and that is the way Alex and his mates intend it to remain. But one may guess that the legend demonstrates that the forefathers of the tribe knew the concern and attraction dolphins seem to have for humans.

Dolphin Rain Dance

Katharine K. Wiley

Rain-wet pink dolphins
amid bright flowered trees
in golden waters

Among the trees we swim,
yes

In shallow days we keep the course
chasing little fish
singing

But in the deep days
ah
then the true song begins
the song of us

Our gray-skinned cousins dance
in the open river water
leaping like the little hatchet-fish

We like to leap
but better the twisting dance
my sisters and daughters about me
pink-fleshed in black-gold water
spinning among the tree tops
the maze dance
about the branches
that waved beneath the sun
and now bow beneath the waters

Our gray-skinned cousins help
the brown-hued land-swimmers
chasing fish to the edges
but where they stop
we begin
the dance of our before-kindred
the dance of our children
and their children
amid the tangled
flower-jeweled branches
the rain dance of pink dolphins
in golden water

Susie Saves Kevin

Richard O'Barry

It's common for dolphins to help one another. That's the way they're brought up. If a dolphin is sick or injured, other dolphins help him stay at the surface of the water so that he can breathe. I have seen dolphins keep other dolphins at the surface of the water long after they have died. When baby dolphins are born (tail first so that they won't drown), the mother dolphin and attending midwife dolphins push the baby to the surface for its first breath of air. It should not be strange that they would help humans the same way. Sailors have always told stories of dolphins saving drowning men by pushing them to shore.

But I never saw anything like that myself—except once.

Art McKee had brought his family out to see me and Susie at the Seaquarium. Kevin, Art's son, was about five years old then and was wandering out on the dock to look for Flipper. Art and I were standing off to the side, Art facing Flipper's Lake and keeping an eye on Kevin. I was facing Art. We were talking about something—probably gold—when all of a sudden, the unflappable Art McKee got a look of horror. I turned. Kevin had slipped and fallen in. But before any of us could move, Susie had pitched the child back onto the dock.

She did this—no doubt of that. But why she did it is the important question. To me it's simple. She did it for the same reason you or I would have done it: to save the child.

In a Wild, Watery Realm

Natasha Nowakowski

"Look! Dolphins!"

My friend Bill is frantically pointing to a crowd of seabirds diving into the blue-green water 50 yards away. At first, all I see are birds, but seconds later, five sleek gray-backs leap and twist elegantly into view. Not believing it, I race my sea kayak closer for a better look, and sure enough, there are five dusky dolphins indulging in a feeding frenzy with a flock of gannets. It was a riveting sight, and it was moments before I realized I was forgetting to breathe.

The circus of dolphins and gannets began to move northward, presumably following the school of blue cod lurking below. Bill and I decided to tag along, and much to our delight, the dolphins acknowledged our presence. Unafraid, the six-foot-long creatures flirted with our sea kayaks, jumped high in synchronized pairs and waltzed through the cloistered waters of the Marlborough Sounds of New Zealand.

Within a few too-short minutes, the dolphins swam off, but we caught up with them two miles later as they fed again, and dallied with us again. Then they departed, for good, leaving us with a memory and their stardust.

Dolphin Games

Richard O'Barry

The story is told, for example, about a man at another aquarium who used to watch the dolphins underwater from a viewing port. The man was smoking a cigarette when a baby dolphin swam up to the port and gazed out. The man nonchalantly blew a puff of smoke at the baby dolphin. The dolphin swam away to his mother, got a mouthful of milk and came back to the port, then blew the milk out at the man, making the same white, puffy cloud with the milk that the man had made with the smoke.

Scraps Gives Back

Mark D'Ambrusio

In 1988 my wife Caron and I spent 10 weeks cruising the lower Caribbean. A gentle sweeping arc took us and two parrots from the Grenadines to Belize aboard our Cheoy Lee 44, roaming on the way through the Venezuelan Islas Los Roques, where the weather and fishing were spectacular.

One day, we decided to explore some nearby sand flats and a fringe reef by dinghy, maybe go around to windward and drift-fish across the flats for bonefish.

Caron got her rod set up while I searched for signs of fish. Suddenly she said, "I saw a big school feeding, near the base of that pole sticking out of the water, 60 yards ahead."

The trades were steady at 12 knots, which precluded a leisurely drift, so we paddle-sailed toward the pole. When we were 30 yards from it, the water exploded in a boiling frenzy. Then I saw the fin.

"SHARK!" I yelled.

Caron grabbed the binoculars, and as she watched, the water exploded again, this time more violently. Then we heard the whistle. It took 10 seconds for us both to reach the same conclusion because we both said at once, "DOLPHIN!"

Still watching through binoculars, Caron said, "Mark, I think it's stuck. At least it hasn't moved since we got here." The bottle-nosed dolphin raised its head out of the water and shouted, presumably to us, "Wee-aht, wee-aht, wee-aht." We decided to get a little closer.

At 10 yards away, the dolphin raised its head again and whistled. "I think that means, 'close enough, people,'" Caron said. I dropped the anchor and we came up with a plan. Below us was about three feet of water with a clear run to open ocean. I'd start the outboard, idle it, and we would drift in to inspect. If the animal became aggressive, we'd exit at full throttle.

Our adrenal glands were in overdrive while we tried to slow the drift with our hands. Ten feet away from the pole, the motor stalled. "You going to start it?" Caron whispered, sweat streaming down her face. "Not yet," I whispered back. Without the motor, the only sound was the dolphin breathing. As we floated past the pole the dolphin brought one eye out of the water and watched.

"I saw a baitfish net wrapped around its tail," I said. "Me too," Caron agreed, "and a white cord, nylon braid. I thought part of it was pink. Maybe it's cut into the fluke—not deep, but probably painful."

Conventional Wisdom says: Don't try to help a wounded wild animal, especially not an animal of this size.

Short on conventions of any sort, we decided to try: idle the motor, drift downwind, grab the pole, free the dolphin. Any trouble and we'd run.

The plan worked. Caron grabbed the pole and I cut the net away while the dolphin just stood there, so to speak. I pulled the cutaway fishnet into the dinghy and the dolphin swam away. The whole rescue took less than 15 seconds.

The next morning, I was fixing a wobbly charcoal grill and Caron was sunning in the cockpit when we heard it: "Wee-aht, wee-aht." Before long, Caron was hanging through the lifelines, petting the dolphin on the forehead. It swam, did some low jumps, and even raised its tail out of the water, seemingly to show us the cut was healing.

A while later, Caron asked, "Did you leave the winch handle in the dinghy?" I checked the two holders.

"Nope, they're secured," I replied.

"Then what's that?" she asked, pointing.

"It's a winch handle," I said. While we were having this exchange, the dolphin rose out of the water with a green glass beer bottle in its mouth. It rested its chin on the side of the inflatable for a moment and dropped the bottle in the dinghy. The first day we got: One slightly corroded winch handle, one red plastic sandal (minus the toe straps), and the green glass beer bottle.

The next day we did even better: Another green glass beer bottle, a four-inch stainless steel pin to something, a white ceramic coffee mug (encrusted), and a large gold coin. Each time the dolphin brought us something we'd jump up and down and applaud wildly. Thank God it was a secluded anchorage; we must have looked like lunatics. By dinnertime the dolphin had a name: Scraps.

On day three the call, "Scraps is back!" went out six times. We got a length of PVC pipe, a glass instrument dome, two aluminum beverage cans (small applause), a wire door to a fish trap (no applause), and a gold medallion with a cut emerald in it (big applause).

The next morning we had to sail on to meet friends in Bonaire. Scraps was a little confused when we put the dinghy on davits, but with a wave and a flip we said goodbye.

We never miss when we tell people how we met our most unique cruising friend, especially when Caron ducks down below to retrieve the gold medallion from its hiding place. Thanks again, Scraps, wherever you are.

Dolphins in Blue Water

Amy Lowell

Hey! Crackerjack—jump!
Blue water,
Pink water,
Swirl, flick, flitter;
Snout into a wave-trough,
Plunge, curl.
Bow over,
Under,
Razor-cut and tumble.
Roll, turn—
Straight—and shoot at the sky,
All rose-flame drippings.
Down ring,
Drop,
Nose under,
Hoop,
Tail,

Dive,
And gone;
With smooth over-swirlings of blue water,
Oil-smooth cobalt,
Slipping, liquid lapis lazuli,
Emerald shadings,
Tinting of pink and ochre.
Prismatic slidings
Underneath a windy sky.

Part Three

Gifts of the Dolphins

What's next in our relationship with our watery alter egos? At the edge of the future we see a hint of what's possible between us in the many dolphin-human therapy programs. There is still plenty of controversy over *what* interacting with a dolphin can do for an injured person and *how* the dolphin does it. But one thing is certain: these accounts show that, wild or captive, dolphins feel a deep sympathy for people and as deep an interest in helping us.

Beyond that, how far can our relationship with dolphins go? Included are a few wilder possibilities.

Dr. Dolphin

Why Does Swimming with Dolphins Help Humans Heal?

Richard Blow

David Cole knows that people consider him a little odd. Cole spends much of his free time swimming with dolphins, and he has enough perspective to realize that this makes him, by most people's standards, eccentric. He doesn't mind.

Cole, a 28-year-old computer scientist, lives about half an hour south of Los Angeles. With excitable gray eyes and long brown hair in ringlets, he looks a little like a youthful Michael Bolton. Cole works for a computer hardware manufacturer, but in his spare time he heads the AquaThought Foundation, a cadre of computer wizards, doctors, and naturalists researching "dolphin-assisted therapy."

For about two decades, physical therapists and psychologists have argued that swimming with dolphins can help the sick and handicapped. Dolphin-assisted therapy seems to accelerate the vocal and physical development of autistic and mentally retarded children, for example. Some researchers claim that dolphin swims also boost the human immune system. Most proponents of the therapy say it helps patients' psychological well-being; the dolphins distract them from their suffering.

But Cole doesn't buy this conventional wisdom. He rejects the idea that dolphins make humans feel better simply by making them happy. That's what clowns are for. Cole believes that swimming with dolphins can have a profound physiological effect on humans. The health of your immune system, the state of your brain, the makeup of your cells—these things, Cole believes, can be radically altered by dolphins.

To the layperson, all this might sound a little nutty. (Acquaintances who knew I was working on this article kept making "Flipper" jokes.) But then, black holes and cloning and artificial intelligence seemed nutty, too—except to the people who believed in them, and who turned one day from daydreamers into visionaries.

A self-described "neurohacker," Cole is a new kind of scientist: a layperson who studies dolphins and neurology not with a degree in marine biology or medicine but with a computer. Like any scientific novelty, Cole isn't always taken seriously. He gets a lukewarm and sometimes hostile reception from the practitioners of orthodox medicine. "It's way too esoteric for a lot of them," he admits.

On the other end of the spiritual spectrum, Cole has to deal with New Agers, some of whom argue that dolphins are really angels or extraterrestrials sent to enlighten humans. "When you look at alternative medicine," Cole says, "New Agers have always been there, drawing discredit to everything in that realm. But there's no replacement for scientific method."

With that, Cole asks me to try Cyberfin, a "Virtual reality interaction" he invented to simulate swimming with dolphins. Eventually he hopes to make Cyberfin realistic enough to substitute for the real thing, helping humans who can't afford a dolphin swim and obviating the need for captive dolphins.

Cole has fashioned his prototype from a converted flotation tank in his garage. Three-D goggles strapped around my head, I lie down on a water mattress inside the tank. Directly overhead is a television monitor; ambient, surreal music pulses from speakers. I feel a little silly, like I'm about to fight the Red Baron, but I try to keep an open mind.

The screen lights up, and suddenly I'm floating in a pool. Two dolphins cavort in the water, zipping by one side of me, a stream of bubbles in their wake. Their whirs and clicks surround me. As I watch, my skepticism fades into curiosity and wonder. One of them swims directly up to my face, and instinctively I shake my head, thinking I'm about to be bumped. Then, with a flip of its tail, the dolphin disappears.

Ordinarily, I would never admit this. But I find myself hoping that it will come back soon.

Cole grew up in Winter Park, Fla., not far from NASA. After graduating from the University of Central Florida in 1988, he founded a software company called Studiotronics. A year later, Cole hooked up with a group that was conducting dolphin-assisted therapy with cancer patients. They told Cole that the dolphins seemed to have a profound effect on the mental states of their patients; Cole offered to perform neurological tests to see what was going on.

"At first I thought our equipment was not working," Cole remembers. "We were using a fairly conventional statistical evaluation of EEG—'This is your brain, this is your brain on dolphins.' The level of change was like nothing I'd ever seen."

Essentially, Cole found a far greater harmony between the left and right sides of the brain after a subject swam with dolphins—a crude suggestion that the brain is functioning more efficiently than normal.

When Cole studied the medical literature to try to explain this phenomenon, he couldn't find anything.

So in 1991 Cole sold Studiotronics to a Japanese company called Chinon, moved to California, and founded AquaThought with a colleague. Though he now works for Chinon, the company gives him all the time he needs to pursue his dolphin research. To facilitate that research, he and a colleague invented a device called MindSet. Looking like a bathing cap with electrodes attached to it, MindSet translates brain waves into real-time images; the fluctuating brain waves are projected onto a computer screen, and the resulting picture bears some resemblance to a lava lamp. The pair created the device because they couldn't afford a $75,000 EEG.

Three years after founding AquaThought, Cole thinks he has figured out why dolphins have beneficial effects on humans. He warns, however, that a lot of people aren't going to believe what he has to say.

Cole isn't the first freethinker to be obsessed with dolphins. He's a disciple of futurist writer and scientist John Lilly, who in 1975 founded the Human/Dolphin Foundation to explore the possibility of interspecies communication. (Lilly himself believed he was following in the footsteps of Aristotle, who had an interest in dolphins.) The dolphins he was studying, Lilly wrote in his 1978 work "Communication between Man and Dolphin," "would do anything to convince the humans that they were sentient and capable."

The field of dolphin-assisted therapy was probably started by Dr. Betsy Smith, an educational anthropologist at Florida International University. In 1971 Smith, who was researching dolphin-human interaction, let her mentally retarded brother wade into the water with two adolescent dolphins. "They were pretty rough dolphins," Smith remembers. But not with her brother. "The dolphins were around him, still, gentle, rubbing on him." Somehow, they knew he was different.

There are now 150 dolphin-assisted therapy researchers worldwide, and there seems little doubt that dolphin swims can help humans with disabilities such as Down's syndrome, autism, depression, attention deficit disorder, muscular dystrophy, and spinal cord injuries. Mentally retarded children who swam with dolphins, for example, "learned their lessons two to 10 times faster than in a normal classroom setting," says Chris Harre of the Dolphin Research Center in Grassy Key, Fla.

Other researchers have found that swimming with dolphins boosts the production of infection-fighting T cells. The generally accepted theory is that swimming with dolphins increases relaxation, which helps stimulate the immune system. Such vague psychological explanations drive Cole crazy; he calls them "horseshit" though he's not a very good swearer. Cole doesn't deny that relaxation helps T cell production. ("I could send you to Tahiti for a week, and your T cell count would probably go up," he says.) But Cole believes that relaxation can't explain the changes in brain waves and blood chemistry in humans who've swum with dolphins.

Cole thinks these changes are caused by dolphins' sonar, which they use to scan the water around them. The sonar is incredibly precise; dolphins can "echolocate" a shark half a mile away in the ocean and determine whether its stomach is full or empty—and, consequently, whether it might be feeding.

"The dolphins produce an intense amount of echolocation energy," Cole says. "It resonates in your bones. You can feel it pass through you and travel up your spine."

Cole's theory is too complicated to do justice here, but it goes basically like this: A dolphin's sonar can cause a phenomenon called cavitation, a ripping apart of molecules. (You see it in everyday life when, for example, you throw the throttle of a speedboat all the way down, but the boat doesn't move; for that second, the propeller is cavitating the water.)

"It's very possible that dolphins are causing cavitation inside soft tissue in the body," Cole says. "And if they did that with cellular membranes, which are the boundaries between cells, they could completely change biomolecules." That could mean stimulating the production of T cells or the release of endorphins, hormones that prompt deep relaxation.

Someday, Cole says, scientists may be able to replicate dolphin sonar and use it in a precise, targeted way to bolster the immune system. But for now, he says, "the dolphin is a part of the experience."

In the cloudy water, I hear the dolphins before I see them: whirs, clicks, and buzzes fill the water.

To find out what it's really like to swim with dolphins, I have come to Dolphins Plus in Key Largo. It's a family-run place, surprisingly small, a suburban house that borders a canal with several large holding pens fenced off. (The dolphins can swim in the canal, but they always return to the pens.) Half an hour in the water costs $75, but before we can take the plunge we are given some guidelines. We are asked not to touch the dolphins; if they want to, they will touch us. We should swim with our hands at our sides, and avoid swimming directly at or behind the dolphins, which they might interpret as hostile. Dolphins generally like children best, women after that, and men last.

Equipped with flippers, mask, and snorkel, I slide off the dock. I can see only a few yards in the murky water. I am so nervous that I worry I won't be able to breathe through the snorkel, but my breath eventually settles into a steady rattle.

Quickly come the dolphin noises, seeming to feel me out. Still, I see nothing. Suddenly, there is a flash of white and gray to my side; a few moments later, a dolphin passes below me. It looks even larger in the water than it does on the surface.

The next time one passes, I dive down. As instructed, I try to make eye contact; for a few seconds the dolphin and I are swimming eye to eye, looking at and—I would swear to it—thinking about each other. These are not just cute, lovable puppy eyes; there's an intelligence here.

More dolphins swim by me, moving too fast for me to keep up. As they swim, huge yet graceful in the water, I am acutely aware of my human clumsiness, and grateful that these animals are letting me swim with them. I can't resist the temptation to wave slowly, hoping that they'll understand the gesture. (This is not so bad: One woman sang "Happy birthday, dear dolphin" through her snorkel for her entire half hour.)

The dolphins swim so close that I'm convinced I'll bump into them, but somehow they always keep an inch, two, three, between us. The temptation to touch them is great, yet resistable. Corny as it sounds, I want them to like me. To touch them would be like coughing at the opera.

At one point I am swimming with a mother and calf; the mother makes eye contact with me, and suddenly I feel it: the zap of the dolphin echolocating me, almost like an electric shock. This, I decide later, is what telepathy must feel like: You hear a sound in your head, but it didn't get there through your ears. It startles me, and I stop swimming. The dolphin opens her mouth, seeming to smile, and she and her calf dart away.

When I get out of the water after 30 fleeting minutes, I feel an incredible calm. I wonder if there is a purely psychological explanation—the magic of the experience affecting me. But it feels deeper than that. Somehow, my body feels different. At this moment, I think David Cole is right.

A woman who was swimming with me sits down. She puts her face in her hands and begins sobbing quietly. "I thought I would be all right," she says to a companion. I never do find out what she means.

Not everyone likes the idea that swimming with dolphins helps humans. Animal rights groups are concerned that such a theory could lead to an explosion in the number of captured dolphins. "We don't feel it's right," says Jenny Woods of People for the Ethical Treatment of Animals. "The animal has to be caged for the program to work."

Cole and other dolphin researchers share this concern. Betsy Smith, for example, has given up swimming with captive dolphins and now only swims with dolphins in the wild. (One concern of Smith's is that echolocation is less common among captive dolphins. When I tell her that I was echolocated, she says the dolphin must have found something about me interesting. "That's flattering," I remark. "Not necessarily," she says. "It may have been a tumor.")

For his part, Cole is trying hard to perfect Cyberfin, so people can virtually swim with dolphins.

Smith and Cole may be racing against time. As more and more people hear of dolphins' therapeutic effects, the desire to exploit the animals for a quick buck will spread.

But to Cole, this is not a reason to stop working with dolphins. He wants to establish a permanent dolphin research facility, something that doesn't exist right now, "We're not looking for a magic bullet," Cole says. "We're looking for ways of interfering with the progression of disease. It's virgin territory."

And if it means that people think he's a little odd—well, David Cole can live with that.

Living by Water

Brenda Peterson

Thrilling, this underwater ballet, as I twirled with the
dolphin, my hands along her flanks. Fluid, this liquid
life below where all is weightless and waves of warmth
enfold my body as I breathed air in this watery element.
And I was not alone. Everywhere was sound—my nieces'
singing and the dolphins' dialogue. My mind suddenly
filled with pictures. Then I realized that every time I
imagined this dolphin doing something, a split second
later she did it. It was not a performance at my request;
it was an answer to my wondering. Call and response. It
was also an anticipation of my delight, a willingness
that is the purest form of play.

I pictured myself spinning round, one hand on
Niki's heart—it happened. I saw both my arms out-
stretched, a dolphin's dorsal offered each hand—and
suddenly I was flying between Niki and Dreamer. It was
impossible to tell who was sending whom these pictures.

But they all happened. It was like instant replay of everything imagined. And now I understood why the child in me chose dolphins. What more perfect playmates?

Ahead in the water swam my sister. Paula was galloping with another dolphin, and my niece Lauren had a dolphin gently resting a long beak on her legs like a paddle to push her through the water. Distracted, I broke one of the basic rules: I got too close to a dolphin and her favorite toy (Paula). Suddenly a wallop to my shoulder. My world turned upside down, and though I was face-up in the air, I breathed water. Sputtering, I broke another rule: my body tilted vertically, a sign to the dolphins of distress. Another whack of a pectoral in the lower back, then a beak thrust under my bottom to raise me above the water.

"Horizontal!" the researchers yelled. "They think you're drowning."

I would rather play with a dolphin than be rescued by one. Those whacks are painful reprimands, a lesson in life and death to a wayward human. Blowholes fiercely expelled their air everywhere around me. Surrounded by all three dolphins, I started to cry. I failed, I felt. I was a fool. And for the first time ever, I was afraid of them.

It was hard not to cower there in the water with them. All the pictures flooding my mind overwhelmed me, and I couldn't figure anything out. Except I remembered to float, though my body was rigid and what I most would have liked to do was curl up into a fetal ball and be safe on shore, the way long ago I'd surface from my own darker daydreams to find myself at the comfortingly ordinary dinner table I first sought to escape. But this was real; I couldn't imagine my way out of it. Or could I?

Again and again one picture appeared in my head. It was I, still shaken, but surrendering to all three dolphins at once. I breathed raggedly, the snorkel like an intruding fist into my mouth. But after closing my eyes, I allowed it. Yes, they could come back and find me again where I floated in fear. At first Niki and Sara were tentative, their beaks very gently stroking my legs. Now that I wasn't going to drown, would I play with them again?

I am small, I thought, and hoped they could hear. *I am just a human being—afraid and fragile in your element. Be careful with me?*

And they were. Together the three of them floated me so slowly my body barely rippled water. Then began the deepest healing. Dreamer gently eased me away from the others with a nudge of her dorsal fin. Her eyes steadily held mine as she swam gracefully in wide arcs of figure eights around the lagoon. In and out through warm water. My body surrendered to the massage, not of hands, but of water and sound. I thought of the others who come here who are not as healthy as I—autistic and Down's Syndrome children, the handicapped, the terminally ill, all of them nursed by the dolphins who embraced me. Deeper than the play, more moving than the sense of another mind in these waters, is the simple kindness of the creatures. I do not understand it. I want to.

When I closed my eyes, the pictures grew stronger, as did my senses. My hands slid down Dreamer's silken body, memorizing notches and scars as a blind woman does her loved one. I remembered that in China those born blind were believed to be the most gifted masseurs—because hands are another way of seeing. My hands still hold the exact feel of dolphin skin. Even now, across time and continent, my hands can still grow warmer, tingle with the memory of that cool, sleek skin that trembles when touched.

Dreamer's name comes from her eyes. Half-lidded, there is in her mild, dark eyes a different light. Sloe-eyed, they call it down South—and the sweet, fizzy drink made from those black sloe berries is a euphoric mix reminiscent of humid, fragrant southern nights. *Down home*, I thought, as I glided through dark green depths. I closed my eyes and felt that this underwater world, too, was down home.

The Boy Who Talked with Dolphins

Paula McDonald

It began as a deep rumble, shattering the predawn silence. Within minutes on that January morning in 1994, the Los Angeles area was in the grip of one of the most destructive earthquakes in its history.

At Six Flags Magic Mountain theme park, 20 miles north of the city, three dolphins were alone with their terror. They swam frantically in circles as heavy concrete pillars collapsed around their pool and roof tiles crashed into the water.

Forty miles to the south, 26-year-old Jeff Siegel was thrown from his bed with a jarring thump. Crawling to the window, Jeff looked out at the convulsing city and thought of the creatures who mattered more to him than anything else in the world. *I've got to get to the dolphins*, he told himself. *They rescued me, and now they need me to rescue them*.

To those who had known Jeff from childhood, a more unlikely hero could not have been imagined.

Jeff Siegel was born hyperactive, partially deaf and lacking normal coordination. Since he couldn't hear words clearly, he developed a severe speech impediment that made it almost impossible for others to understand him. As a preschooler, the small sandy-haired child was taunted as a "retard" by other kids.

Even home was no refuge. Jeff's mother was unprepared to deal with his problems. Raised in a rigid, authoritarian household, she was overly strict and often angry at his differences. She simply wanted him to fit in. His father, a police officer in their middle-class Los Angeles community of Torrance, worked extra jobs to make ends meet and was often gone 16 hours a day.

Anxious and frightened on the first day of kindergarten, five-year-old Jeff climbed over the schoolyard fence and ran home. Furious, his mother hauled him back to school and forced him to apologize to the teacher. The entire class overheard. As the mispronounced and barely intelligible words were dragged out of him, he became instant prey for his classmates. To fend off the hostile world, Jeff kept to isolated corners of the playground and hid in his room at home, dreaming of a place where he could be accepted.

Then one day when Jeff was nine, he went with his fourth-grade class to Los Angeles's Marineland. At the dolphin show, he was electrified by the energy and exuberant friendliness of the beautiful animals. They seemed to smile directly at him, something that happened rarely in his life. The boy sat transfixed, overwhelmed with emotion and a longing to stay.

By the end of that school year, Jeff's teachers had labeled him emotionally disturbed and learning disabled. But testing at the nearby Switzer Center for children with disabilities showed Jeff to be average-to-bright, though so anxiety-ridden that his math-test score came out borderline retarded. He transferred from the public school to the center. Over the next two years he became less anxious, and his academic achievement improved dramatically.

At the start of seventh grade he returned, unwillingly, to public school. Tests now showed his I.Q. in the 130s, the gifted range. And years of therapy had improved his speech. But to classmates Jeff was still the same victim.

Seventh grade was unfolding as the worst year of Jeff's life—until the day his father took him to Sea World in San Diego. The minute the boy saw the dolphins the same rush of joy welled up in him. He stayed rooted to the spot as the sleek mammals glided past.

Jeff worked to earn money for an annual pass to Marineland, closer to his home. On his first solo visit, he sat on the low wall surrounding the dolphin pool.

The dolphins, accustomed to being fed by visitors, soon approached the astonished boy.

The first to swim over was Grid Eye, the dominant female in the pool. The 650-pound dolphin glided to where Jeff was and remained motionless below him. *Will she let me touch her?* he wondered, putting his hand in the water. As he stroked the dolphin's smooth skin, Grid Eye inched closer. It was a moment of sheer ecstasy for the young boy.

The outgoing animals quickly became the friends Jeff had never had, and he began to live from visit to visit. And since the dolphin area was isolated at the far end of Marineland, Jeff often found himself alone with the playful creatures.

One day Sharky, a young female, glided just below the surface until her tail was in Jeff's hand and then stopped. *Now what?* he wondered. Suddenly Sharky dived a foot or so below the surface, pulling Jeff's hand and arm underwater. He laughed and pulled back without letting go. The dolphin dived again, deeper. Jeff pulled back harder. It was like a game of tug-of-war.

When Sharky surfaced to breathe, boy and dolphin faced each other for a minute, Jeff laughing and the dolphin open-mouthed and grinning. Then Sharky circled and put her tail back in Jeff's hand to start the game again.

The boy and the 300- to 800-pound animals often played tag, with Jeff and the dolphins racing around the pool to slap a predetermined point, or giving each other hand-to-flipper high-fives. To Jeff, the games were a magical connection that he alone shared with the animals.

Even when there were summer crowds of 500 around the pool, the gregarious creatures recognized their friend and swam to him whenever he wiggled his hand in the water. Jeff's acceptance by the dolphins boosted his confidence, and he gradually emerged from his dark shell. He enrolled in a course at a nearby aquarium and devoured books on marine biology. He became a walking encyclopedia on dolphins and, to his family's amazement, braved his speech impediment to become a volunteer tour guide.

In 1983 Jeff wrote an article for the American Cetacean Society's newsletter, describing his experiences with the Marineland dolphins. He was unprepared for the result: embarrassed by the extent to which he'd been playing with the dolphins without the park's knowledge, Marineland management revoked his pass. Jeff returned home numb with disbelief.

For their part, Jeff's parents were relieved. They could see no benefit to the time their strange, misfit son was spending with dolphins—no benefit until a day in June 1984 when Bonnie Siegel took an unexpected long-distance phone call. That evening she asked her son, "Did you enter some kind of contest?"

Sheepishly Jeff confessed that he'd written an essay for a highly coveted Earthwatch scholarship worth more than $2000. The winner would spend a month in Hawaii with dolphin experts. Now, telling his mother about it, he expected a tirade. Instead she said quietly, "Well, you won."

Jeff was ecstatic. Best of all, it was the first time that his parents realized he might achieve his dream of someday sharing his love of dolphins.

Jeff spent the month in Hawaii, teaching strings of commands to dolphins to test their memories. In the fall, he fulfilled another condition of the scholarship by giving a talk on marine mammals to fellow students at Torrance High School. Jeff's report was so enthusiastic that it earned him, at last, grudging respect from his peers.

After graduation, Jeff struggled to find work at various marine-research jobs, supplementing the low pay with minimum-wage moonlighting. He also obtained an associate's degree in biology.

In February 1992, he showed up in the office of Suzanne Fortier, director of marine-animal training at Six Flags Magic Mountain. Though holding down two jobs, he wanted to do volunteer work with Magic Mountain's dolphins on his days off. Fortier gave him the chance—and was immediately amazed. Of the 200 volunteers she'd trained in ten years, she'd never seen anyone with Jeff's intuitive ability with dolphins.

In one instance, her crew needed to move a sick 600-pound dolphin named Thunder to another park. The animal had to be transported in a nine-by-three-foot tank. During the journey, Jeff insisted on riding in the truck bed with Thunder's tank to try to calm the anxious animal. When Fortier later called from the cab of the truck to ask how Thunder was doing, Jeff replied, "He's fine now. I'm cradling him." *Jeff's actually in the tank with Thunder!* Fortier realized. For four hours, Jeff floated inside the cool tank, holding Thunder in his arms.

Jeff continued to amaze his co-workers with his rapport with the animals. His favorite at Magic Mountain was Katie, a 350-pound, eight-year-old dolphin who greeted him exuberantly and swam with him for hours.

Once again, as at Marineland, Jeff could interact with the dolphins and find affection in return. Little did he dream how severely his love would be tested.

As Jeff struggled to reach Magic Mountain on the morning of the earthquake, freeways were collapsing, and caved-in roads often forced him to backtrack. *Nothing is going to stop me*, he vowed.

When Jeff finally reached Magic Mountain, the water in the dolphin pool was halfway down the 12-foot-deep pool, and more was draining steadily from a crack in the side. The three dolphins there when the quake hit—Wally, Teri and Katie—were in a frenzy. Jeff lowered himself to a ledge five feet down and tried to calm them.

To ease the dolphins through the continuing tremors, Jeff attempted to distract them by playing games, but it didn't work. Worse, he had to reduce their food: the pool's filtration system had shut down, creating the additional risk that an accumulation of their body waste would further contaminate the water.

Jeff remained with the dolphins that night as temperatures fell into the 30s. He was still there through the next day, and the next, and the next. Other staffers trickled in and prepared to move the dolphins.

On the fourth day a road opened, and staffers secured a truck to transfer Wally, Teri and Katie to the dolphin pool at Knott's Berry Farm. But first, someone had to get them into their transport tanks.

Transporting a dolphin is normally a routine procedure, after it has been safely guided through a tunnel and hoisted on a canvas sling. But the water level in the connecting tunnel was too low for the animals to swim through. The three dolphins would have to be caught in open water and then maneuvered into canvas slings.

Staffer Etienne Francois and Jeff volunteered for the job. As much as he trusted the dolphins, Jeff knew the likelihood of getting hurt or bitten by them in an open-water capture was almost 100 percent.

Wally was easily removed from the pool, but Teri and Katie became erratic. Each time Jeff and Etienne closed in on Katie, the powerful dolphin fended them off with her hard, pointed beak.

For almost 40 minutes the men struggled as Katie butted and whacked them with her thrashing tail. Finally, just before they maneuvered her into a sling, she sank her needle-sharp teeth into Jeff's hand. Ignoring the bleeding, Jeff helped capture Teri and hoist her into the transport tank.

When the dolphins reached Knott's Berry Farm, Katie was exhausted—but calmer. Later, Fortier told friends that Jeff's courage and leadership had been essential in safely transporting the dolphins.

Today, Jeff is a full-time dolphin trainer at Marine Animal Productions in Gulfport, Miss., where he organizes programs for schools.

One day, before he left for Mississippi, Jeff gave a demonstration to 60 children from the Switzer Center at one of the aquariums where he had taught. He saw that a boy named Larry had slipped off to play alone. Realizing Larry was an outcast, as he himself had been, Jeff called him forward and asked the boy to stand next to him. Then Jeff plunged his arms into a nearby tank and hauled out a harmless but impressive three-foot horn shark. As the children gasped, he allowed Larry to carry the dripping creature proudly around the room.

After the session, Jeff received a letter reading: "Thank you for the magnificent job you did with our children. They came back glowing from the experience. Several told me about Larry getting to carry the shark. This was probably the happiest and proudest moment of his life! The fact that you were once a student here added to it. You are a model of hope that they, too, can 'make it' in life." The letter was from Janet Switzer, the center's founder.

For Jeff, that afternoon held an even more gratifying moment. As he spoke, he saw his mother and father in the audience, watching intently. From the look on their faces, Jeff could tell they were proud of their son at last.

Jeff has never earned more than $14,800 a year in his life, yet he considers himself a rich man and an exceptionally lucky one. "I'm completely fulfilled," he says. "The dolphins did so much for me when I was a child. They gave me unconditional love. When I think about what I owe the dolphins. . . ." His voice trails off momentarily, and he smiles. "They gave me life. I owe them everything."

The Dolphin

Geoffery Moore

If I could just be a dolphin,
I'd have the whole sea to show off in.
Through the air I would sail,
Then I'd walk on my tail.
I'm afraid I would show off quite often.

True Friends
A Free-Swimming Dolphin
Stays Close to Her Human Pal

Laura Daily

Five years ago a fisherman named Abeidalla Mekiten spotted a sleek, gray creature swimming near his fishing boat. It was a bottlenose dolphin. Over the next few days, Mekiten, a Bedouin tribe member who lives in Nuweiba, Egypt, watched the creature patiently. What happened next changed the fisherman's life. He decided to dive into the water for a closer look. To Mekiten's surprise the dolphin didn't flee. Instead she cautiously eyed him. Day after day the two swam until one morning the dolphin, which Mekiten calls Olin, let the fisherman touch her. A lasting friendship began between the wild, free dolphin and the young man.

Tourists now visit Nuweiba for a chance to swim alongside the wild dolphin. They must be careful not to get too close because Olin is not always as friendly with strangers as she is with Mekiten. The tourists pay a small fee to the people of Nuweiba, bringing much-needed money to the very poor village.

Most dolphins live in family groups called pods. Occasionally a dolphin is forced out of its pod by other members. "Those that are thrown out may not want to be alone," says Oz Goffman, a marine biologist at the University of Haifa in Israel. He studies the friendship between Mekiten and Olin. Lone dolphins may "replace the companionship of the pod with that of human beings."

Such behavior may explain why Olin, completely free to swim away, has stayed near Nuweiba.

Once in a while Olin joins a passing dolphin pod for a few days, but she always returns to the waters off Nuweiba. During a visit with other dolphins in 1997, Olin became pregnant. A year later she gave birth to a male calf. Now Mekiten plays with mother and baby.

Says Goffman, "Human-dolphin friendships are rare, but this is obviously a friendship Olin wants or she would leave." So far Olin seems content to stay.

Dolphins Study War No More
They Mend Nerves

Michael Specter

There was a dark time, not so long ago, when it seemed as if the killer dolphins of the Black Sea Fleet would never find peace without war.

Trained, in the words of a Ukrainian Navy spokesman, to "seek, find, kill," the 70 special forces dolphins lost their sense of purpose when the wall fell.

Like John le Carre, another cold-war superstar knocked off balance by a world of freedom, the dolphins couldn't seem to get the point of the watery universe if sniffing out mines—and occasionally exploding them—was no longer necessary.

"When the cold war ended we thought about everything," said Capt. Nikolai Savchenko, the chief spokesman for the Ukrainian Navy. "We tried to persuade oil companies to retrain them. But nobody was interested. In a way, it was your typical case of defense conversion. These dolphins were raised in a world that had ceased to exist."

Well, sort of. Speaking purely in evolutionary terms, dolphins were never meant to be fitted with headgear and loaded into special cages where they could dive hundreds of feet in search of mines and foreign frogmen. But these animals clearly performed way beyond Darwin's expectations.

"You can't really call them animals," said Dr. Lyudmila Lukina, a physician who runs a program using the dolphins in a new role: therapy for children with autism and other problems. "They are far too smart for that."

When the dolphins found enemy mines they would simply attach a special glue to the metal (with a gentle nose kiss) that let Soviet sappers, who could blow them up, know where they were. It is unclear if this ever actually happened. Captain Savchenko asserted that the dolphins were even occasionally dropped from helicopters with parachutes—although the purpose for this type of mission is impossible to divine.

Scientists would travel here from across the Soviet Union to study dolphin behavior and try to figure out better ways to make use of their unusual intellectual gifts. But in this city, where every job had some military purpose, the Ukrainian Navy was left bankrupt after the Soviet Union dissolved in 1991.

Soon the dolphins—who can live to the age of 55 and eat more than 30 pounds of fish a day—were on the edge of starvation. The base here had all but ceased to function. Stipends had disappeared. Dozens of warships bobbed hopelessly on the edge of the sea. Then somebody had the therapy idea.

It was not such a radical notion. Dolphin therapy has been used for years in countries like Israel, Japan and the United States. Because dolphins are highly sophisticated and intelligent, most physiologists and researchers believe they are better able to communicate with humans than any other species—although their nickname is still only man's second best friend.

"They work with all sorts of children," said Svetlana Matyshovna, a marine physiologist on the base who supervises some of the dolphins' new activities. "Autistic children, shy children. Dolphins can cure many different problems. They make people feel at home. They improve their auras."

Their what?

"Auras," said Mrs. Matyshovna, a 29-year veteran of research here, who also said she had studied levitation and the effect of U.F.O.'s on the population, in addition to her dolphin work. "The field around a person that permits him to live and breathe freely," she said, matter-of-factly. "That is his aura."

Oh, that. Mrs. Matyshovna whipped out a metal wire with a wooden handle. It looked exactly like what you do to a hanger when you lock your keys in your car and you have to break in—and she pointed it at, among others, this correspondent. It started to twirl wildly when she stuck it about four inches from my chest.

"Very low aura," she muttered. "If you spent some time swimming with the dolphins it would improve immediately."

Perhaps, but we will never know. (Actually, the man who took the picture for this article did jump in with one of the dolphins. His aura was good to begin with and, according to Mrs. Matyshovna's gyrating wire, it got much better after 10 minutes clinging to the dorsal fin of the sleek, wet dolphin.)

Dr. Lukina said dolphins could cure bed-wetting, dissipate anxiety, help mute children speak. She said the program had only about 20 dolphins now, and she was unwilling to discuss whether their military research continues.

She could not account for the absence of the other dolphins in the original program and, although two buses full of youngsters passed by, the staff was unwilling to make them available to talk about their experiences.

"This is a private sensation," she said, standing on a rotting pier and tossing cod at her charges. She regularly turns away rich Russians, usually vacationing nearby in Yalta, who want to swim with the dolphins.

"Whatever these dolphins did before was serious business," she said. "But now it's serious too. We have a goal here, and it's about learning and healing. And that is a miracle because for years this was a secret base where nobody could come. Now we have found a new purpose to our work. And so have the dolphins."

Maritime Moocher
Marine Biologists Have His Number, But Dolphin 56 Won't Stop Hustling for Handouts

Pam Lambert

As sleek and as swift as a submarine, the voracious creature closes in on his unsuspecting prey—a fishing boat somewhere in the Atlantic Ocean, a few miles off Florida. Suddenly, surging toward the surface, he sticks his bottle-like snout out of the water just inches from the side of the boat, flashing his trademark wide, toothy grin. The fishermen are startled at first, then amused. They toss him some bait or maybe a sandwich.

Meet the infamous Dolphin 56, the Bart Simpson of his breed. All along the East Coast, his eating habits are giving indigestion to marine biologists, conservationists and government fisheries agents. In fact, Dolphin 56 has become, as one biologist puts it, the poster boy for bad dolphin behavior. When federal authorities put out their press releases warning boaters against feeding marine mammals, his mug shot is right at the top.

"There are myriad reasons not to feed the wild dolphin," says Trevor Spradlin, a marine mammal biologist for the National Marine Fisheries Service, whose national Don't Feed the Dolphins campaign, underway since 1993, is designed to end the free lunch for Dolphin 56 and others of his ilk—a wily bunch who have been known to pry open crab traps to filch herring and chicken parts. "First and foremost, it harms their health and welfare. We have reports of people feeding dolphins everything from junk food to firecrackers."

In addition to the obvious dietary dangers, say Spradlin and other scientists, dolphins also run the risk of getting sick from contaminated bait, losing the ability to forage for themselves and being slashed by propellers when they get too near boats. And the animals aren't the only ones putting themselves in harm's way with the feedings, which have been illegal since 1991. (Maximum penalty: a fine of up to $20,000 and as much as a year in jail.) "People have been injured—dolphins can become aggressive," says Keith Rittmaster, natural science curator for the North Carolina Maritime Museum, noting that the mammals can—and do—bite. Spradlin concurs. "Our culture has promoted the idea that dolphins are Flipper," he says. "That's just a myth."

The fisheries education effort—which has included public-service announcements, brochures and even

"Don't Feed the Dolphins" Frisbees—couldn't have found a better poster boy than Dolphin 56. During the two decades since he was first captured as a 12-year-old in Florida's Indian River Lagoon and branded on his dorsal fin (with painless frozen liquid nitrogen) for a federally funded study headed by research biologist Dan Odell, the bottlenose has become a veritable highwayman of the high seas, migrating as far north as New York while trawling for treats. . . .

"I know it's 56 long before I get a look at his dorsal fin because of his behavior," says Rittmaster. "Typically he's surrounded by a group of boats." Adds biologist Spradlin: "56 is not a bad dolphin. He's behaving in this fashion because people have trained him to do so." Biologists suspect he first turned to begging in his home lagoon, where fishermen often toss their old bait to dolphins.

Spradlin and the network of researchers monitoring 56 are the first to admit they are perplexed by many aspects of his behavior. "Why did he leave Florida?" asks Odell. "Was he kicked out of the group? I have no idea." One thing the experts agree on, though, is that 56 is no dummy. "One time he begged and we didn't feed him," recalls Rittmaster. "Then he appeared on the surface with a 10- to 12-in. mullet in his mouth. Was he saying, 'Look, if you're going to be so stingy,

I don't need you, I can catch fish on my own'? Or was he saying, 'Hey, this is what I want you to give me'?"

"He's perfectly capable of feeding himself, but that takes more work," observes Odell, now working at SeaWorld in Orlando. "If you could convince people not to feed him, that would help reform him." Well, maybe. "He's been doing this for decades," Odell concedes with a shrug. "I don't know if he's reformable or not."

Dolphin Therapy—Making a Splash

Kelly Milner Halls

Dingy (*DING-ee*) tried all her tricks to get Joseph La Nave's attention the first day he visited her tropical home. She exploded out of the lagoon, her smooth body shimmering in the sun, before crashing back into the water. But Joseph ignored the dolphin.

As Dingy vanished beneath the saltwater surf, Joseph's parents wondered if they had made a mistake. They'd brought their physically challenged son to the Dolphin Human Therapy and Research Program in Key Largo, Florida. They wanted Joseph to be around dolphins before he worked with one in a therapy class. How could Dingy or any of the other dolphins help Joseph if he didn't take notice?

Dingy, however, wouldn't give up. A few minutes later, she popped out of the water with a sea bean clenched between her teeth. With one motion, she flipped the bean directly into Joseph's lap.

Startled, Joseph looked up and locked eyes with Dingy. It was instant love.

Joseph's mom and dad asked Dingy's trainers, "Why did she give Joseph a soggy sea plant?"

"She wanted to make eye contact with Joseph," they said. To do so, Dingy had given Joseph her dolphin calf's favorite toy. "And that may have seemed like the only way to do it."

Physically challenged kids who ignore things around them will work extra hard to earn a little time with any dolphin, says Dr. David Nathanson, program director. The program uses dolphins to help children explore abilities they've not yet tested.

Because Joseph was born with cerebral palsy, a disorder that affects muscle control, he can't speak.

"We read his gestures, smiles, and facial expressions," his dad explains. Maybe dolphin therapy would help Joseph break through a barrier.

When six-year-old Joseph returned for his therapy class, he was holding his sea bean souvenir. Squirt was now his dolphin teacher instead of Dingy, but Joseph was still excited.

Joseph's physical therapist, Louellen Klints, watched him closely. She was trying to decide how to set goals for Joseph.

By the next day, Louellen knew what to do. As Joseph floated on a dock, she asked him to point to a picture that matched the word she said. "Joseph, where is the star?" his teacher asked again and again. "Can you touch the star?" As Joseph reached out and touched it, everyone got excited.

"Way to go!" Louellen cheered. "How about a foot kiss from Squirt?"

With a grin, Joseph dipped his toes into the warm water. Squirt swam to him and nuzzled his foot.

"Match a few more pictures, and you can go in the water with her," his teacher said.

Joseph did more than that. He spoke his first word—"in." He had asked to get in the water with Squirt!

Wearing wet suits, Joseph and Louellen slipped into the water and signaled for Squirt. The eight-foot-long dolphin glided next to them. It waited as the pair took hold of its dorsal fin.

"Joseph had a look of joy," his father recalls. "He loves rides—the rougher, the better. Joseph's smile said, 'I'm a little afraid, Dad, but I'm loving it.'"

Will Joseph's dolphin experience carry over into his life in New York? It's possible, says Sherry Stephens, mother of twelve-year-old Brooke, a dolphin therapy graduate.

"Brooke has a confidence she didn't have before," her mom explains. "The dolphins helped her believe she could do it. Brooke knows now that she can do other things, too."

Joseph's dad agrees. "The therapists here have asked Joseph to dig down inside himself and pull something out that hasn't been seen before."

"We didn't come here to see Joseph cured," his dad says. "We came for a breakthrough on which we could build. And Joseph would tell you—the dolphins definitely helped."

A Diver's Dream

Bonnie J. Cardone

Twelve years ago Howard Hall wrote an article for *Skin Diver* entitled "Playing Tag with Wild Dolphins." In it he recounted a four hour game of keep away, played with Spotted Dolphins and a red scarf in The Bahamas. The photo illustrating the article showed five dolphins just below the surface, looking expectantly at the camera. The red scarf floats in the water right in front of them. Obviously, the camera man is "it!"

This is the kind of magical encounter divers dream of and, from the moment I read article, I, too, wanted to live that dream. It finally happened last summer, aboard the Sea Fever.

At least two pods of Spotted Dolphins roam a pair of shallow sandbanks known as White Sand Ridge, off the northwest end of Grand Bahama Island. The pods have been interacting with humans for more than 20 years. (The Sea Fever's owner/captain, Tom Guarino, was among the first to snorkel with them some 23 years ago.) I believe the dolphins have trained us quite well.

The area they roam is quite large and the Sea Fever applies two methods of finding them. Occasionally the boat anchors in an area the dolphins are known to frequent and waits for them to appear. Most of the time, however, the boat cruises a wide area, looking for the dolphins. When they want to be found, they swim near the surface, often announcing their presence by jumping the boat's wake. Sea Fever's guests wait for word from the captain, then eagerly abandon ship to join the dolphins. The water is shallow, usually less than 30 feet deep, and very warm, about 84°F. No one uses scuba, it makes us way too slow. Instead, we use fins, masks and snorkels. Many free-dive, but even those whose ears cannot withstand a week of continuous ups and downs will get good photos staying right on the surface.

Many times the encounters are brief. The dolphins swim at a leisurely but steady pace, trailed by pale skinned finners. I think they find it amusing to have us following them. They could easily swim faster, they could easily choose some other route, but they choose to swim with humans, just as we choose to swim with them.

Sometimes the dolphins stay around for an hour or even longer. As we watch, they dig in the sand, foraging for Razorfish snacks. They dance, tail down, just above the bottom. They twist and twirl, zoom to the bottom and back to the surface. Through it all, they continually glance our way, just to make sure we're paying attention. On occasion they play keep away with each other, using a strand of Sargassum Weed. We live for the minutes (and sometimes hours) the dolphins linger at the surface in our company, coming within touching distance (although we are cautioned not to touch). Eye to eye with these smiling creatures, who look at us just as curiously as we look at them is, indeed, the stuff of divers' dreams!

A Sense of Unconditional Love

Connie Stribling

I still remember those squeals of delight and water splashing-sounds as my attendant was parking our rental car in the lot of the Marine Mammal Research Center, Dolphins Plus, in Key Largo, Florida. Little did I realize then that those sounds would forever be instilled in my memory as part of what I think was a lifesaving encounter with highly evolved, compassionate and playful dolphins.

After just completing graduate school, I needed a vacation before I was to begin teaching English in an inner-city school in New Orleans. I had heard that swimming with the dolphins would be therapeutic as a stress reducing experience, but I had no idea I was about to embark on probably the most incredible adventure of my life (other than in 1985, tumbling down a mountain one-hundred-fifty feet in a run-away car.) After spending the last five years as a C-6 quadriplegic from somersaulting in that car, coupled with five years in college to become productive in society again, I was overdue for relaxation of any kind. I participated in dolphin research and had an underwater experience that far exceeds relaxation.

As we were leaving a briefing about the dolphins and their environment, we were shown to a separate part of the twelve foot deep basin, which empties into the Atlantic, where the dolphins are periodically let out to sea. In this section of the basin were four female dolphins, Dreamer, Sara, Nicki, and Spunky. I had no idea that I would be able to tell them apart by their personalities! One other woman was a subject of the research and would enter the water simultaneously with my attendant, the researcher, and me. She had suffered a nervous breakdown and had already been there close to a month. She related to me how debilitated she was when she arrived and how rejuvenated she was now. She did not know how to explain her speedy recovery other than to describe a feeling that the dolphins had sensed her emotional distress and being surrounded by a sense of "unconditional love," as many others, including myself, have termed it.

Immediately after I was lowered into the water from a floating pier, I heard the clicking noises, a sound of the dolphins' unique sonar system. Their "clicks" measure distance and energy or electrodynamic fields surrounding any living thing (as verified through Kirlian photography and electronography). Seconds later, two dolphins flashed through the water and gave me a sidelong glance (I was told by a marine biologist on staff that the dolphins were using their sonar to form a hologram in their brain of my entire body including my nervous system and muscular system). Suddenly, a dolphin, Nicki, was making direct eye contact with me, which is an indescribable feeling, except to say that I felt I was looking directly into the eyes of a creature who knew a lot more than I did, coupled with an immeasurable feeling of love surrounding me.

Nicki and Dreamer then began to tap repeatedly on each of my trocanters (my hip bones were protruding because of my stress-induced weight loss.) I was surprised, thinking that they were trying to tell me in their own way that my legs would not move and, as a result, were pushing me through the water.

That was mid-August, 1990. On October 8, 1990 I admitted myself into the hospital, two or three days away from death according to my physician. I had an anaerobic microorganism tunneling from where my trocanters were touching me beneath the skin almost to the bone! Some inner voice kept trying to tell me to remember something, even in the midst of chaos, while teaching. Then, when I barely could hold my head up, much less teach (I was running a temperature of 104 degrees), I remembered the dolphins tapping on my hip bones and I asked myself the question: Could it be that they were trying to tell me there was something more urgently wrong with my body? It was three surgeries later, in mid-February before I was discharged.

An Indescribable Gyration of Synergy

S. Laurance Johnston and Russell Bourne

John Arndt, a paraplegic since 1988, participated in [the Upledger Institute] pilot program. He is an actor, writer, poet, and playwright who once worked with Tennessee Williams. He recorded his experiences with the dolphins in a journal. Following is an excerpt.

"Dolphin therapy this morning; my Lord, what a morning! First we went for a 'structured swim' with two pregnant dolphins. The regular stuff, dorsal pulls, imitative games, kisses, and pets. Then into a pool with a dolphin named Tina, a young female, and a very strong girl. Tina would go to my feet and blast energy up from there; it was completely powerful. Suddenly my feet came alive with a pulsing energy. That pulsing energy went through my body and into my lower spinal cord. Every time Tina would blast from my feet, I would get a 'therapeutic earthquake' from my first lumbar vertebra down into my sacrum. All my tissues in the lower part of my body were literally shaking with energy. Talk about sending a shiver up the spine; this was the ultimate."

Next day: "Starting at my feet, there is a constant flow and movement of impulse, an indescribable gyration of synergy that rotates and pulsates, ebbs and flows, buzzes and beats, vibrates and harmonizes with myriad sensations that move up and down my legs. This is more than I've felt down there since the night I fell out of that tree. And the location is different, too . . . this morning, the energy web has moved all the way down into my feet and pulsated upward from there. It is warm, I would say an almost glowing awareness of my feet and legs, tissues, and bone. It feels so fine."

Running with the Dolphins

Micheal Elliott

I stopped the car beside the sign. "Why do you come all the way to Tybee to run?" I asked before he opened the door, though I didn't really expect an answer.

Surprising me, he turned and spoke in soft, hushed tones. "I like to run with the dolphins."

"What? Run with the dolphins?" I had no idea what he was talking about.

He settled in his seat for a moment and closed his eyes while speaking.

"Sometimes, when it's low tide and the ocean is as slick as glass, I'll run just at the water's end. They are always there, but you can't always see them. I'll be running, and then they surface. If you adjust your pace, you can run with the dolphins all the way down the beach. That's why I run out here."

With that he thanked me and jumped out of the car and began walking the back streets toward the north part of the island. He evidently began his jog at one end of the beach and proceeded to the other. I continued my ride home.

Atlantic bottle-nose dolphins are common to the southeast coast of the United States. This steel-colored species may be seven to twelve feet in length and may weigh up to 500 pounds. With a loud *whoosh*, they hastily inhale air through their blowholes, then submerge their melon-shaped heads. As streamlined as a missile, dolphins cruise the waters looking for squid, fish, and crabs, streaking at twenty to forty miles per hour after their prey.

Dolphins are easily spotted from the shore by beachcombers when the fin breaks the surface. Tourists often mistake them for another kind of fish and scream, "Shark!" to the top of their lungs, causing a minor panic for persons who are visiting the ocean for the first time or who have seen the movie *JAWS* one too many times.

For regular visitors to the sea or those who live on islands such as Tybee, the sight of dolphin pods—a group of four or five swimming together—is a very common sight. Comfortable with the number of swimmers invading their home, dolphins will dart nearby. They are fond of following boats and surfacing at almost arm's length. Occasionally, one will wash up on shore with large chunks of the body having been ripped off by sharks. Dolphins are very common sights on Tybee, so I failed to understand this man's captivation with running beside them. . . .

Several days later I had a very bad time at work. Everything that could go wrong did. I was unable to accomplish much. At every turn some crisis demanded my immediate attention. On top of that, the air conditioner went out at the office, and my suit was soaked with sweat.

The drive from Savannah to Tybee can be very therapeutic on such days. It only takes a couple of minutes to get out of the city via President Street Extension, then past an industrial district, to Whitemarsh Island, to Talahi Island, to Wilmington, and then the seven-mile ride on the causeway through the marshes. By the time I reach the Lazaretto Creek bridge, I felt that an invisible door was closing behind me and the city was left to its own devices until I returned.

Still tense when I got home, I decided to run. Running allows my body to release the stress and tension from the workday. A couple of miles later, I am relaxed enough to have an intelligent conversation with my wife, ask my children how their days were, and begin planning supper.

I changed into my running shorts—interestingly enough manufactured by some company that named them "Dolphins"—put on an old football jersey, and donned my running shoes. I am not one of those runners who makes a fashion statement whenever he jogs. I do not wear anything remotely similar to spandex and never consciously determine whether I am color coordinated or not.

I do not like to run with anyone. I like to set my own pace without having to worry about keeping up or, worse, waiting for someone to maintain my pace. I do not care to have a conversation while I run; I prefer to think about whatever enters my head. I do not keep my time, as some runners do, or have an established course. The only agenda is to run until I feel like stopping. I have found running as a conclusion to my job is a very effective way to separate my work life from my home life.

On this day, I ran north on Butler Avenue, Tybee's main street. It was a hot day with no breeze. The asphalt was blistering, the humidity high, and my pace slow. Eventually, I made the wide turn at the north end of the island and proceeded to the post office, turned right, and jogged to Memorial Park and the baseball field.

I passed the nursing home and entered a new, but not completed, subdivision named Captain's Row. The streets are paved and the lots marked, but there are only a couple of actual houses. I went to the end of the imaginary neighborhood and turned into the sand dunes. The sand held onto my feet as I labored to reach the top and, once there, saw the beauty of the Atlantic Ocean spread out before me. Turning right, I ran down the beach.

I felt healthy and quickened my pace. Each ounce of sweat brought out the frustrations of the day. It felt good to be home. There were few people on the beach. Only an occasional couple would pass me—holding hands, talking, and looking for seashells. The other runners seemed to have chosen to stay on the streets or not run at all because of the ninety-degree temperature. My steps naturally carried me toward the water, where there were no waves—only the soothing lapping of the sea against the shore.

Everything was so still and motionless that I could easily pick them up. Three or four dolphins swam in the same direction I was running. They were near the shore and easily made their way, gliding through the calm waters. They would submerge, travel a distance, and then surface and blow a puff of air from their holes. It seemed as nothing else existed except for the dolphins, the ocean, the sand, and my steps. My pace matched their speed, and together we made our way down the beach.

We were so close I could see their eyes when they surfaced. Dark and delightful, they appeared to hold the dreams of everyone who has ever sailed the seas and know all of the mysteries of the deep. While I knew that the natural curve of their mouths form an upward turn at either end, it seemed they were smiling at me. I felt invigorated. I ran and they swam. I pushed myself to a runner's euphoria while they effortlessly rolled their bodies through the surf.

The south end jetties were in sight. With time running out, I continued to steal glances toward the sea. I was almost at the stopping point; I could not climb the rocks that formed the bulkhead and keep pace. The dolphins would continue into the open sea, and I would have to turn away from them at the jetty. I did not want this experience to come to such an abrupt end.

Ten feet from the jetty, I slowed to a halt, and the dolphins submerged. I cursed and gazed toward the water. Then one dolphin jumped straight up, reaching for the sky and bringing its body completely out of the water. It seemed to be suspended in the air and twisted its torso and flipped. Its head entered the water through the same hole it had created when it jumped out of the water. The rest of the pod surfaced again, blowing the air through their holes and making the loud *whoosh* sound. Then they were gone.

For several minutes I stood gawking at the sea. The words of my runner friend came to me: "I like to run with the dolphins." I knew what he meant and understood why he hitched a ride to Tybee every day just to jog. It made perfect sense.

I have tried to explain the experience to others, but they merely think it was "cute" that I saw dolphins while I was running. They either claim it must have been nice or describe the last time they saw dolphins. These experiences frustrate me, and I no longer attempt to share what it's like to run with the dolphins.

I take solace in an episode in the life of Ernest Hemingway, as described by Arnold Samuelson. Once when sailing his boat, *Pilar*, from Key West to Cuba, he found himself in an enormous school of porpoise that he estimated to be a mile long and four miles wide. Steering the *Pilar* with the porpoise for over an hour, whole smaller schools at times jumped in unison in the almost-purple water. After watching for some time, Hemingway told the others on board not to try and write about what he had seen in a serious way: "Things like this are almost impossible to describe." Sometimes, however, the image has become so much a part of who you are that you cannot help but try.

I still see my friend from time to time. While we do not speak or wave, he seems to have noticed a difference in me. Ever so briefly, he turns his head my way and looks into my eyes. Ever so slightly, a smile graces his lips.

Bibliography

Aristotle. *History of Animals*. Translated by D'Arcy Wentworth Thompson. Oxford, England: Oxford University Press, 1910.

Berry, Adrian. *Galileo and the Dolphins: Amazing But True Stories from Science*. New York: John Wiley and Sons, 1997, pp. 11–13.

Bliss, Yvonne M. Signed deposition of interview. In *Porpoises and Sonar*, by Winthrop N. Kellogg. Chicago: University of Chicago Press, 1961, p. 14.

Blow, Richard. "Dr. Dolphin: Why Does Swimming with Dolphins Help Humans Heal?" *Mother Jones*, January–February 1995, p. 28 ff.

Cardone, Bonnie J. "Bahamas Odyssey: Sea Fever's One on One Adventures with the Spotted Dolphins." *Skin Diver*, May 1998, p. 72 ff.

J. E. Cirlot. *A Dictionary of Symbols*. Translated by Jack Sage. New York: Philosophical Library, 1962, pp. 84–85.

Cochrane, Amanda, and Karena Callen. *Dolphins and Their Power to Heal.* Rochester, Vt.: Healing Arts Press, 1992, pp. 52–53.

Daily, Laura. "True Friends: A Free-Swimming Dolphin Stays Close to Her Human Pal." *National Geographic World.* August 1999, p. 6 ff.

D'Ambrusio, Mark. "Scraps." *Cruising World*, September 1993, p. 160.

Dickens, Charles. *American Notes.* First published 1842. London: Oxford University Press, 1957, pp. 221–22.

Dobbs, Horace. *Follow the Wild Dolphins.* New York: St. Martin's Press, 1982, pp. 64–65.

Micheal Elliott. *Running with the Dolphins and Other Tybee Tales.* Macon, Ga.: Smyth & Helwys Publishing, 1995, pp. 99–103.

Ferguson, George. *Signs and Symbols in Christian Art.* New York: Oxford University Press, 1954, p. 10.

Glueck, Nelson. *Deities and Dolphins: The Story of the Nabataeans.* New York: Farrar, Straus & Giroux, 1965, 1993, pp. 315, 316, 334, 339.

Halls, Kelly Milner. "Dolphin Therapy—Making a Splash." *U.S. Kids*, June 1996, p. 2 ff.

Herodotus. *The History of Herodotus.* Translated by George Rawlinson. London: J. M. Dent & Sons, 1858, 1910, pp. 10–11.

Hesiod. *Homeric Hymns: Epic Cycle: Homerica*. Translated by Hugh G. Evelyn-White. Cambridge, Mass.: Harvard University Press, 1914, pp. 353–59.

Johnston, S. Laurance, and Russell Bourne. "Dolphin-Assisted Healing." *Paraplegia News*, July 1999, p. 17.

Kaiya, Zhou, and Zhang Xingduan. *Baiji: The Yangtze River Dolphin and Other Endangered Animals of China*. Washington, D.C.: Stone Wall Press, 1991, pp. 10–11, 12–15.

Lamb, F. Bruce. "The Fisherman's Porpoise." *Natural History*, May 1954, pp. 231–32.

Lambert, Pam. "Maritime Moocher: Marine Biologists Have His Number, But Dolphin 56 Won't Stop Hustling for Handouts." *People Weekly*, December 6, 1999, p. 145 ff.

Lawrence, D. H. *The Complete Poems of D. H. Lawrence*. Edited by V. de Sola Pinto and F. W. Roberts. New York: Viking Penguin, 1964, 1971.

Lowell, Amy. *Pictures of the Floating World*. New York: MacMillan, 1919, pp. 139–40.

Lucas, F. L. *Greek Poetry for Everyman*. New York: Macmillan, 1951, pp. 237-39.

McDonald, Paula. "The Boy Who Talked with Dolphins." *Reader's Digest*, April 1996, pp. 82–87.

Moore, Geoffery. "The Dolphin." *Jack & Jill*, January–February 1995, p. 26.

Natural History editors. "Saved by a Porpoise." *Natural History*, November 1949, pp. 385–86.

Nowakowski, Natasha. "In a Wild, Watery Realm." *The New York Times*, January 3, 1999.

O'Barry, Richard. *Behind the Dolphin Smile*. Chapel Hill, N.C.: Algonquin Books of Chapel Hill, 1988, pp. 55, 97.

Oppian. "Halieutica." In *Colluthus Tryphiodorus*, translated by A. W. Mair. New York: G. P. Putnam's Sons, 1928, p. 493.

Peterson, Brenda. *Living by Water*. Seattle, Wash.: Alaska Northwest Books, 1990.

Pliny the Elder. "Dolphins in the Roman Province of Narbonne." In *Natural History*, Book IX, translated by H. Rackham. Cambridge, Mass.: Harvard University Press, 1983, pp. 183–87.

Plutarch. "On the Intelligence of Animals." In *Moralia*, Volume XII, translated by Harold Cherniss and William C. Helmbold. Cambridge, Mass.: Harvard University Press, 1957, pp. 471–73.

Reynolds, Susan Lynn. *Strandia*. Toronto, Canada: HarperCollins, 1991, pp. 3–5.

Robson, Frank. *Pictures in the Dolphin Mind*. Dobbs Ferry, N.Y.: Sheridan House, 1988, pp. 28–29, 79–82.

Slater, Candace. *Dance of the Dolphin: Transformation and Disenchantment in the Amazonian Imagination*. Chicago: University of Chicago Press, 1994, pp. 94–98.

Smith, Brian D., Bishnu Bhandari, and Kumar Sapkota. *Aquatic Biodiversity in the Karnali and Narayani River Basins—Nepal*. Kathmandu, Nepal: IUCN, 1996.

Specter, Michael. "Dolphins Study War No More: They Mend Nerves." *The New York Times*, August 4, 1997.

Stribling, Connie. "My Swim with the Dolphins: Is the Media Causing False Hope about Their Healing Powers?" *Accent on Living*, Spring 1994, p. 32 ff.

United Press International. "Comrade Dolphin." *The New York Times*, June 5, 1966.

Permissions

Every effort has been made to contact the owners of copyrights still in effect. The author and publisher gratefully acknowledge and thank the following for permission to use previously published material:

"The Bond Cannot Be Broken: A Folktale from Nepal of the Ganges River Dolphin" excerpted from Brian D. Smith, Bishnu Bhandari, and Kumar Sapkota, *Aquatic Biodiversity in the Karnali and Narayani River Basins—Nepal*. Copyright © 1996 by Brian D. Smith, Bishnu Bhandari, and Kumar Sapkota. Reprinted by permission of the authors.

"How Dolphins Came from People: A Chumash Indian Legend" retold by Katharine K. Wiley. Used by permission of the author.

"How People Came from Dolphins: An Aboriginal Story from North Australia" excerpted from Amanda

For more stories, poems, and folktales about dolphins, please visit the *Lore of the Dolphin* Web site at *www.dolphinlore.com.*

Other Books from
Beyond Words Publishing, Inc.

Listening to Wild Dolphins
Learning Their Secrets for Living with Joy
Author: Bobbie Sandoz
$14.95, softcover

Listening to Wild Dolphins, written by a well-established therapist, chronicles her remarkable and healing experiences while swimming with a pod of wild dolphins off the shores of her Hawaiian home over the past ten years. She has observed that the dolphins have qualities which humans can model to become more balanced and joyful in everyday life.

Dolphin Talk
An Animal Communicator Shares Her Connection
Author: Penelope Smith
$9.95, audiotape

Tales of adventure and communications from the dolphins transport us into the excitement and mystery of our eternal connection with these charismatic marine mammals. Smith shares the dolphin healing journey that enabled her to overcome a lifelong fear of deep water and swim with wild dolphins in the open ocean. Feel the special affection for the human species that the dolphins impart; hear about the merging of dolphin and human consciousness; experience the haunting tones of dolphin "resounding skull bone chanting," creating an opening in the listener's skull to better receive the dolphin's energetic transformations. According to Smith, the dolphins facilitate the weaving of energy matrices of consciousness over our planet, allowing receptive and ready humans to receive the dolphins' pure love throughout their cellular structure and to experience telepathic communication. Feel the dolphins' healing power conveyed through this audiotape, directly by them!

Animal Talk
Interspecies Telepathic Communication
Author: Penelope Smith
$14.95, softcover

If your animal could speak, what would it say? In *Animal Talk*, Penelope Smith presents effective telepathic communication techniques that can dramatically transform people's relationships with animals on all levels. Her insightful book explains how to solve behavioral problems, how to figure out where your animal hurts, how to discover animals' likes and dislikes, and why they do the things they do. Without resorting to magic tricks or wishful thinking, *Animal Talk* teaches you how to open the door to your animal friends' hearts and minds. An entire chapter of this illuminating book is devoted to teaching people how to develop mind-to-mind communication with animals. *Animal Talk* also explores the topics of freedom, control, and obedience; understanding behavior from an animal's point of view; how to handle upsets between animals; tips on nutrition for healthier pets; and the special relationship between animals and children. There is even a section on how to communicate with fleas and other insects!

When Animals Speak
Advanced Interspecies Communication
Author: Penelope Smith; Foreword: Michael J. Roads
$14.95, softcover

In her first book, *Animal Talk*, Penelope Smith confirmed what many people had hoped was true—that we can communicate with our animal friends. *When Animals Speak* takes us to a deeper level as life-changing revelations are communicated directly from the animals. You will discover who animals say they truly are; how they feel about humans and life on earth; how they choose their paths in life and death; what their spiritual understanding and purposes are; and how they can be our teachers, helping us heal ourselves and guiding us back to wholeness. By regaining the language understood by all species, you will laugh and cry as you experience the animals' refreshing, moving, and sometimes startling points of view. *When Animals Speak* will become a treasured key to your own intuitive connection with the rest of creation.

Kinship with the Animals
Editors: Michael Tobias and Kate Solisti-Mattelon
$15.95, softcover

Contributors to *Kinship with the Animals* represent a myriad of countries and traditions. From Jane Goodall illustrating the emergence of her lifelong devotion to animals to Linda Tellington-Jones describing her experiences communicating with animals through touch, the thirty-three stories in *Kinship with the Animals* deconstruct traditional notions of animals by offering a new and insightful vision of animals as conscious beings capable of deep feelings and sophisticated thoughts. The editors have deliberately sought stories that present diverse views of animal awareness and communication.

To order or to request a catalog, contact
Beyond Words Publishing, Inc.
20827 N.W. Cornell Road, Suite 500
Hillsboro, OR 97124-9808
503-531-8700

You can also visit our Web site at *www.beyondword.com*
or e-mail us at *info@beyondword.com*.

Beyond Words Publishing, Inc.

OUR CORPORATE MISSION
Inspire to Integrity

OUR DECLARED VALUES
We give to all of life as life has given us.
We honor all relationships.
Trust and stewardship are integral to fulfilling dreams.
Collaboration is essential to create miracles.
Creativity and aesthetics nourish the soul.
Unlimited thinking is fundamental.
Living your passion is vital.
Joy and humor open our hearts to growth.
It is important to remind ourselves of love.